ANIMALS

COLORING BOOK

FUN FOR KIDS

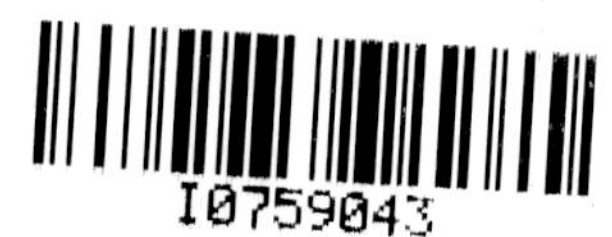

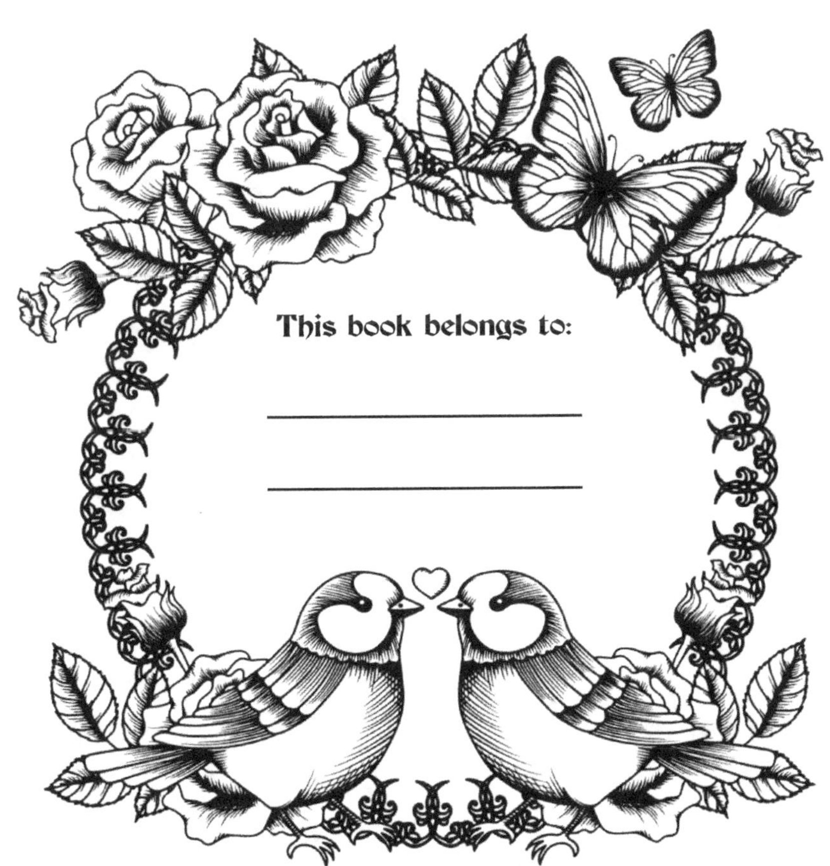

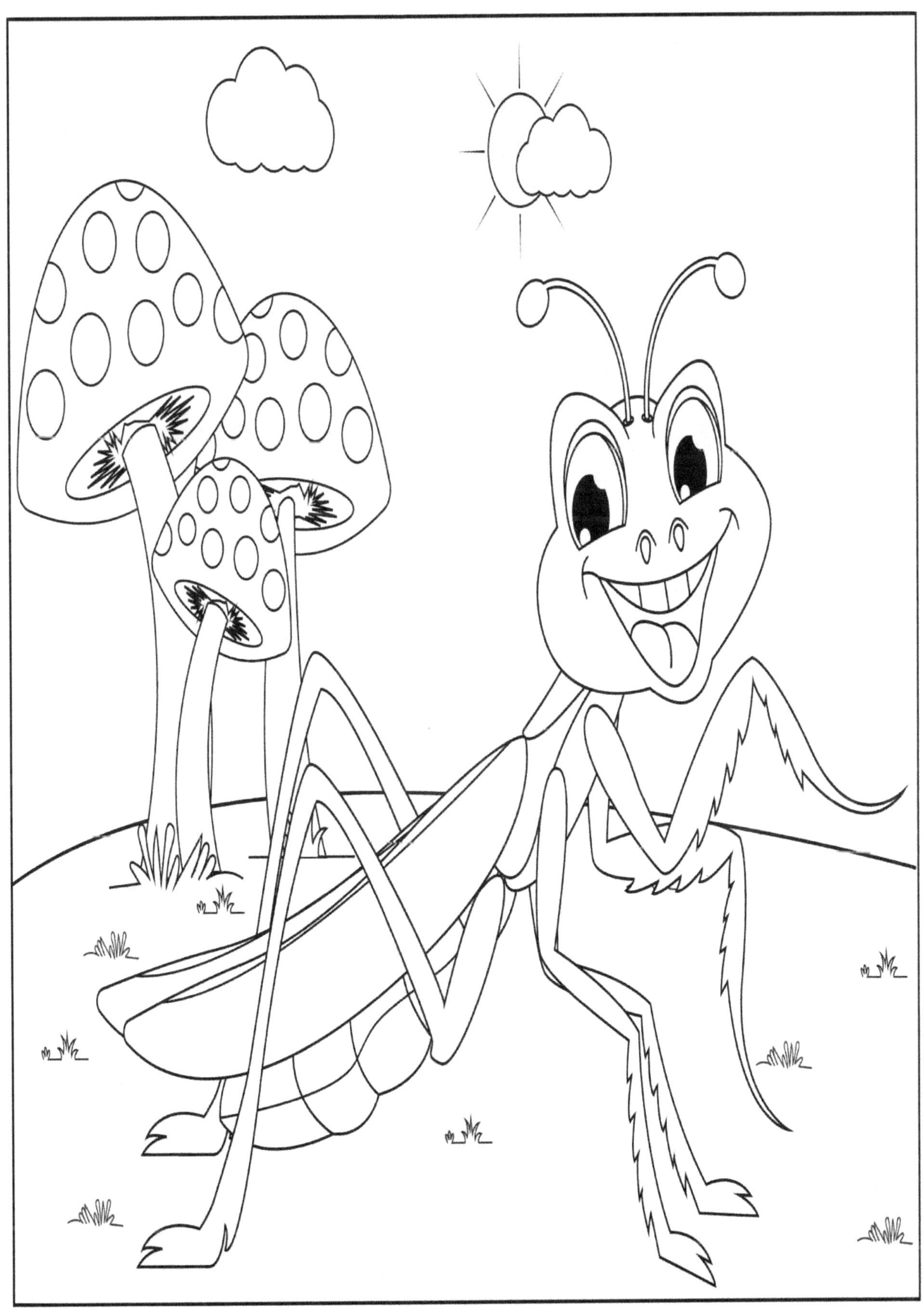

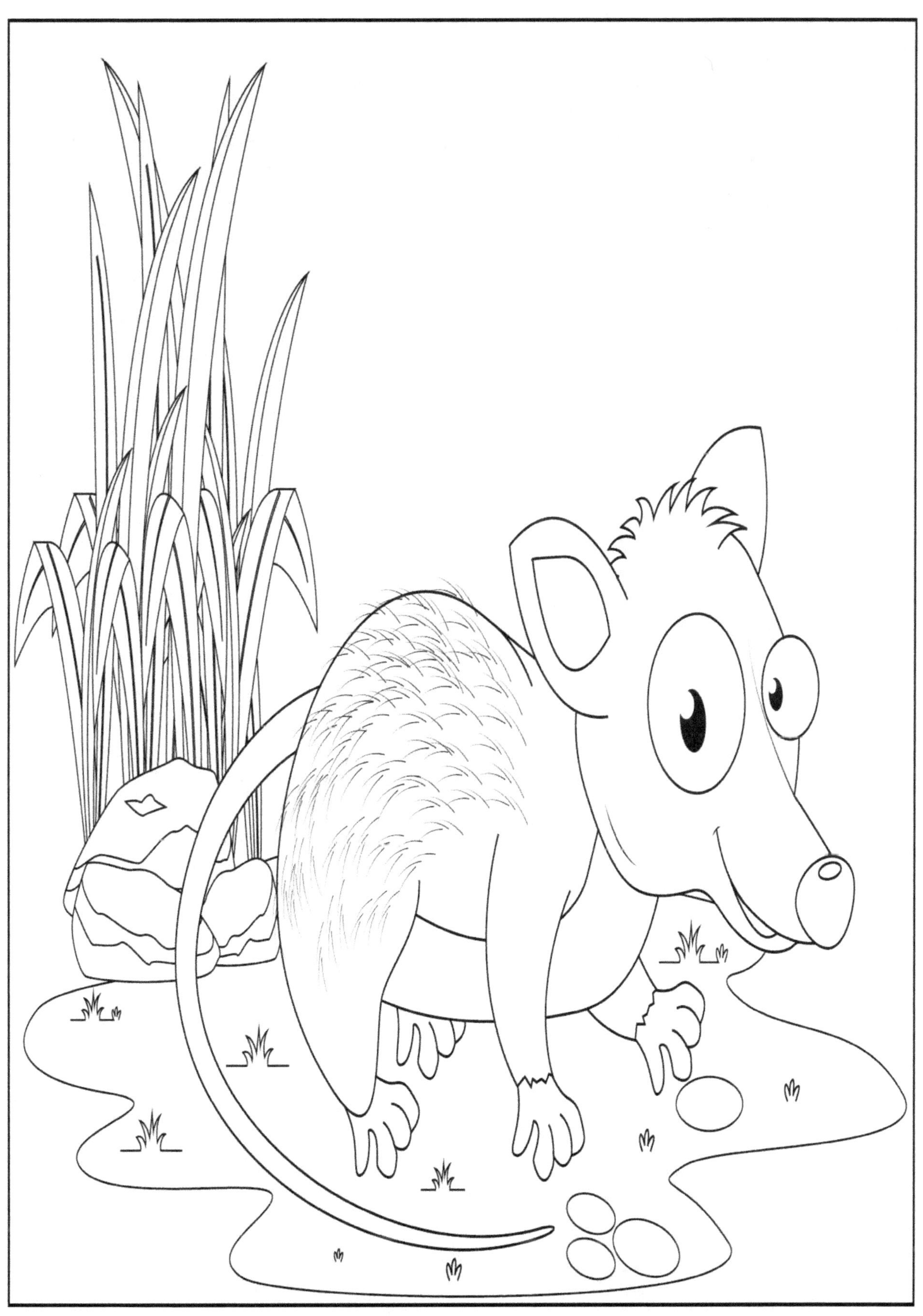

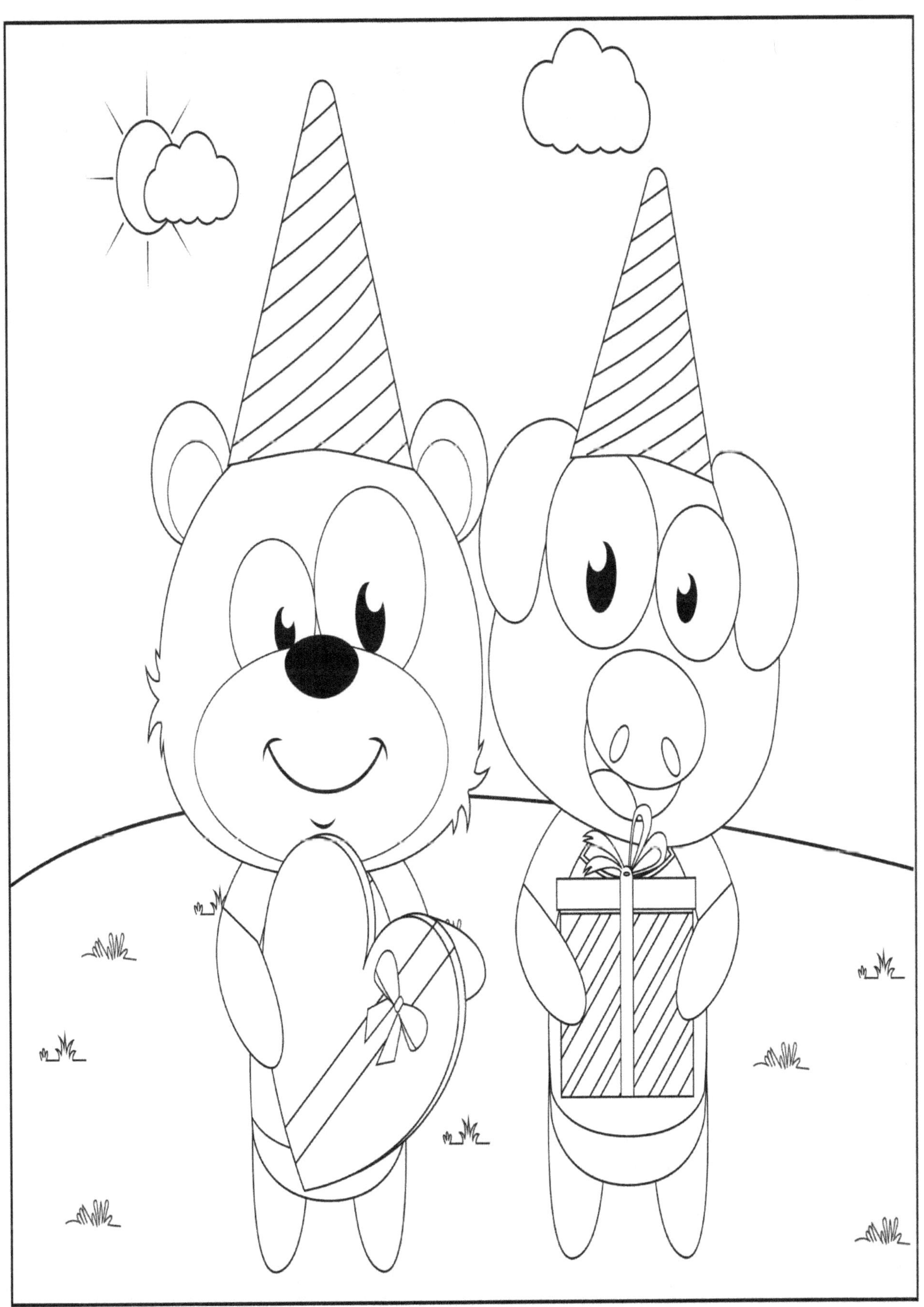

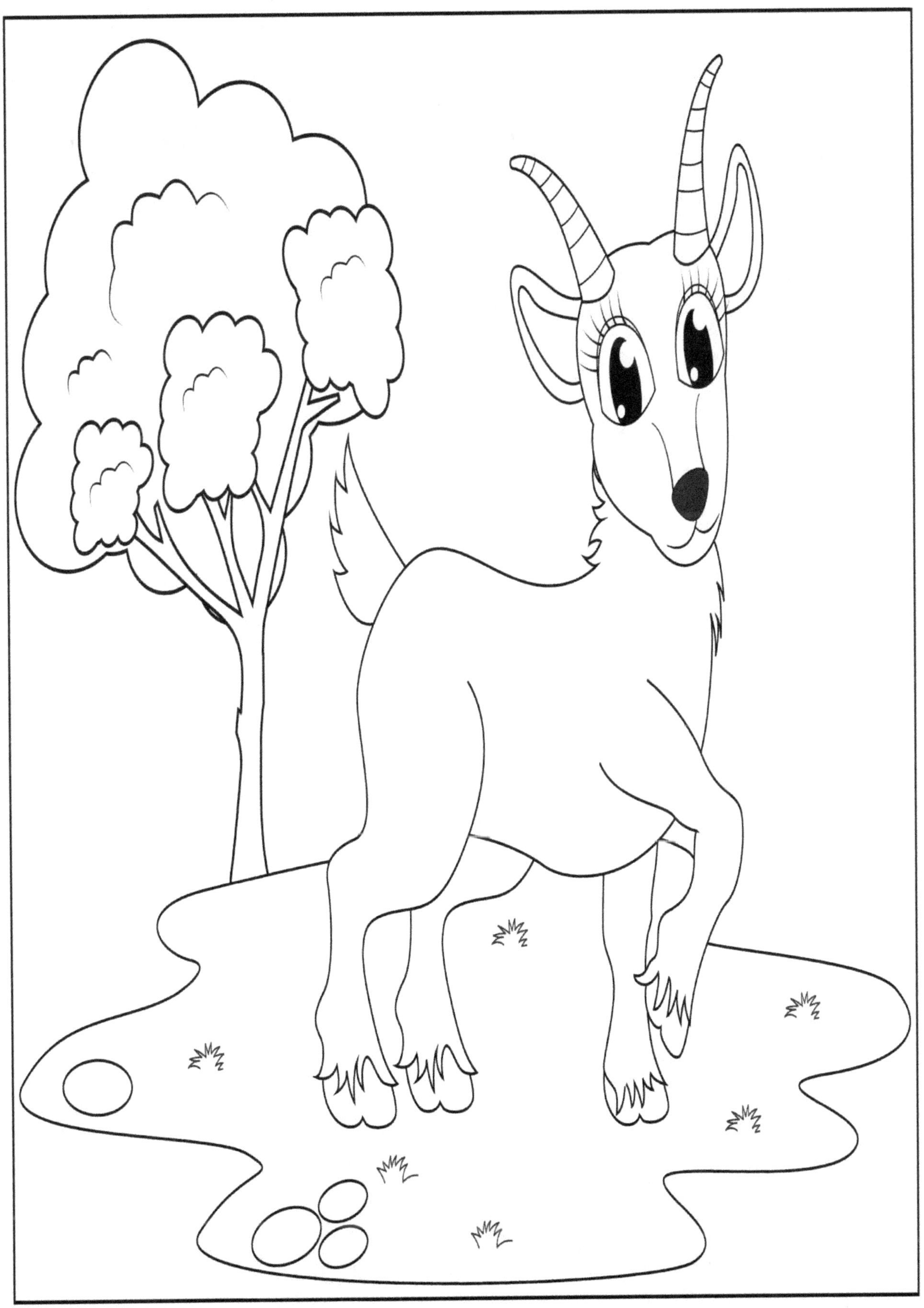

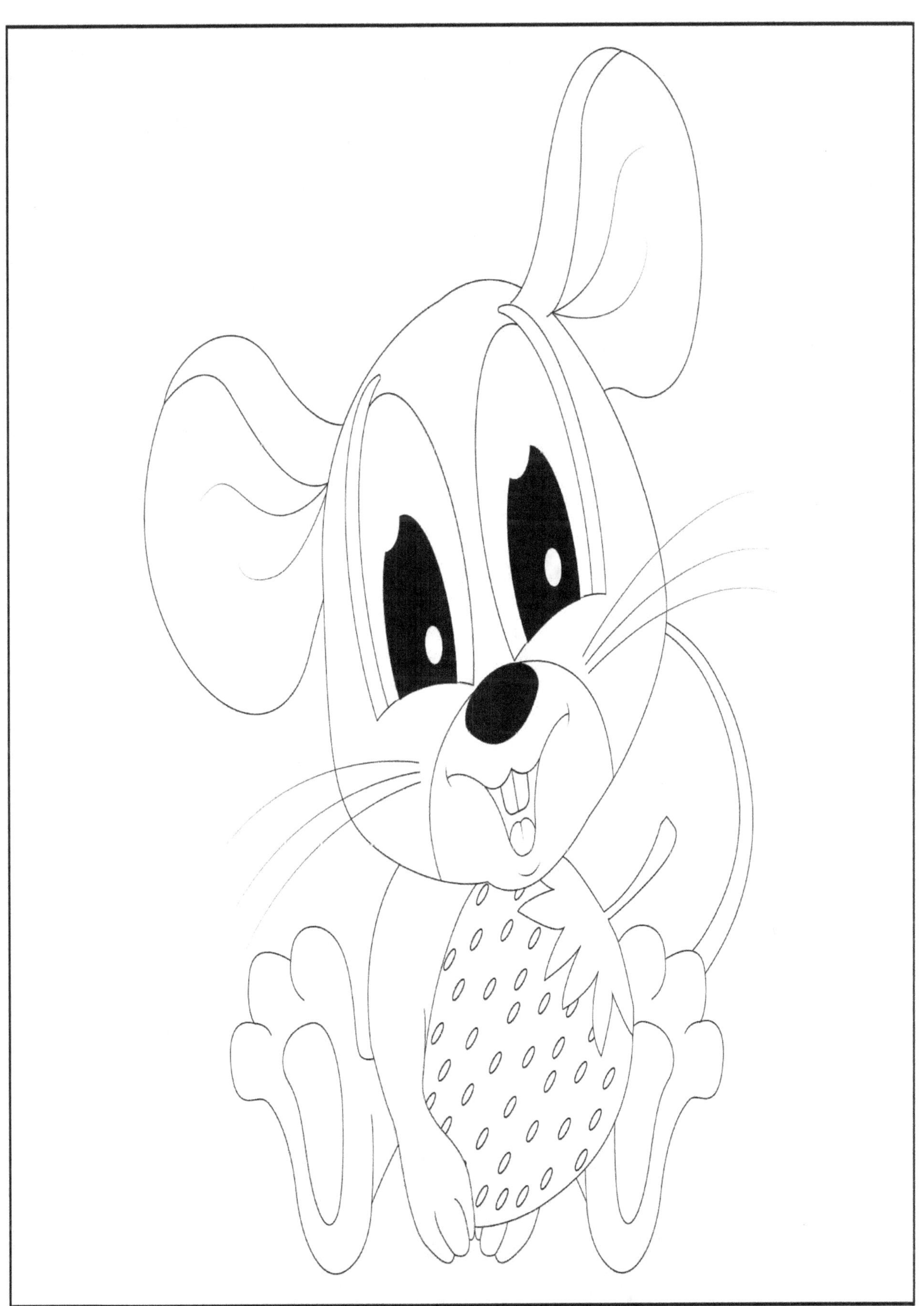

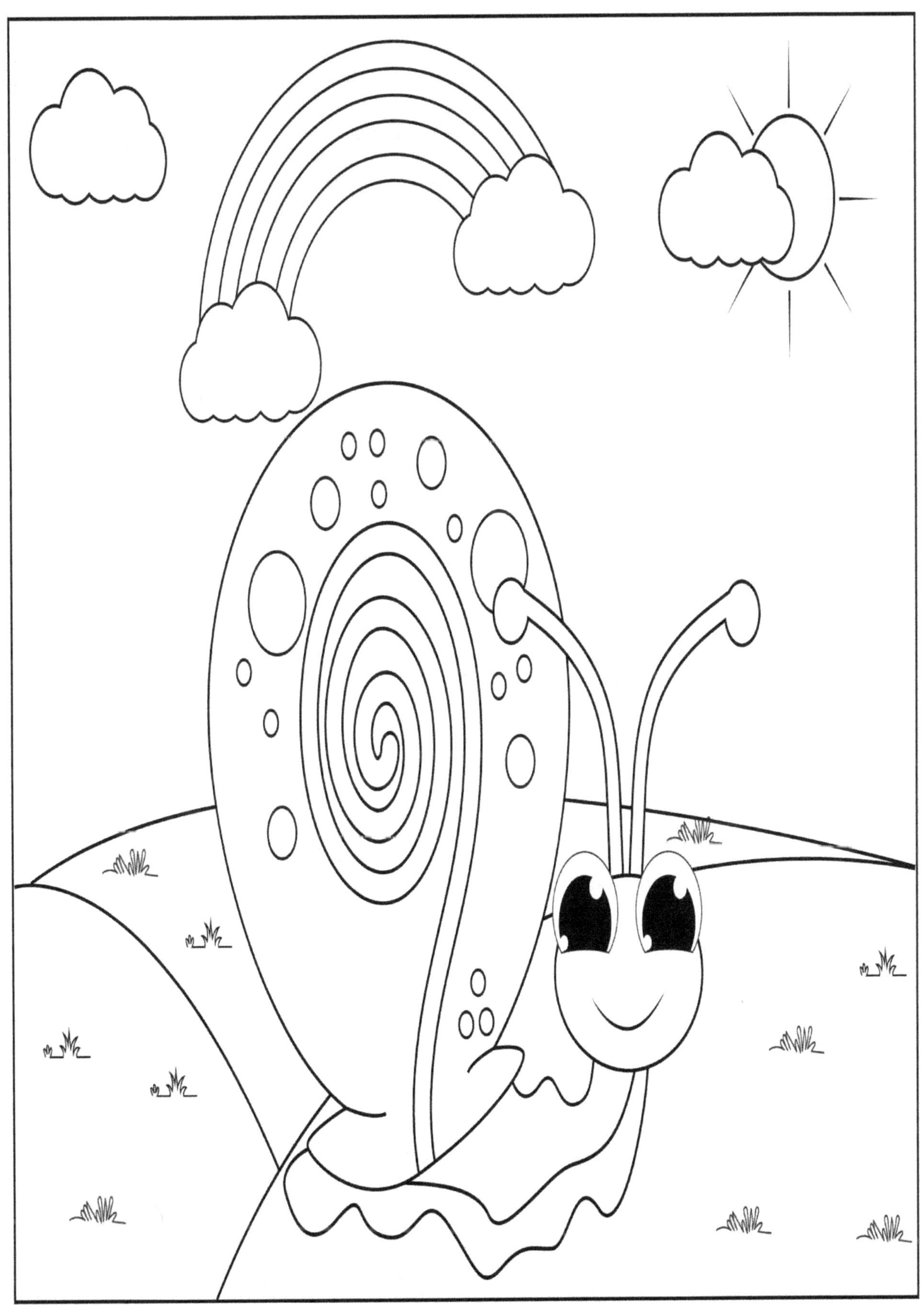

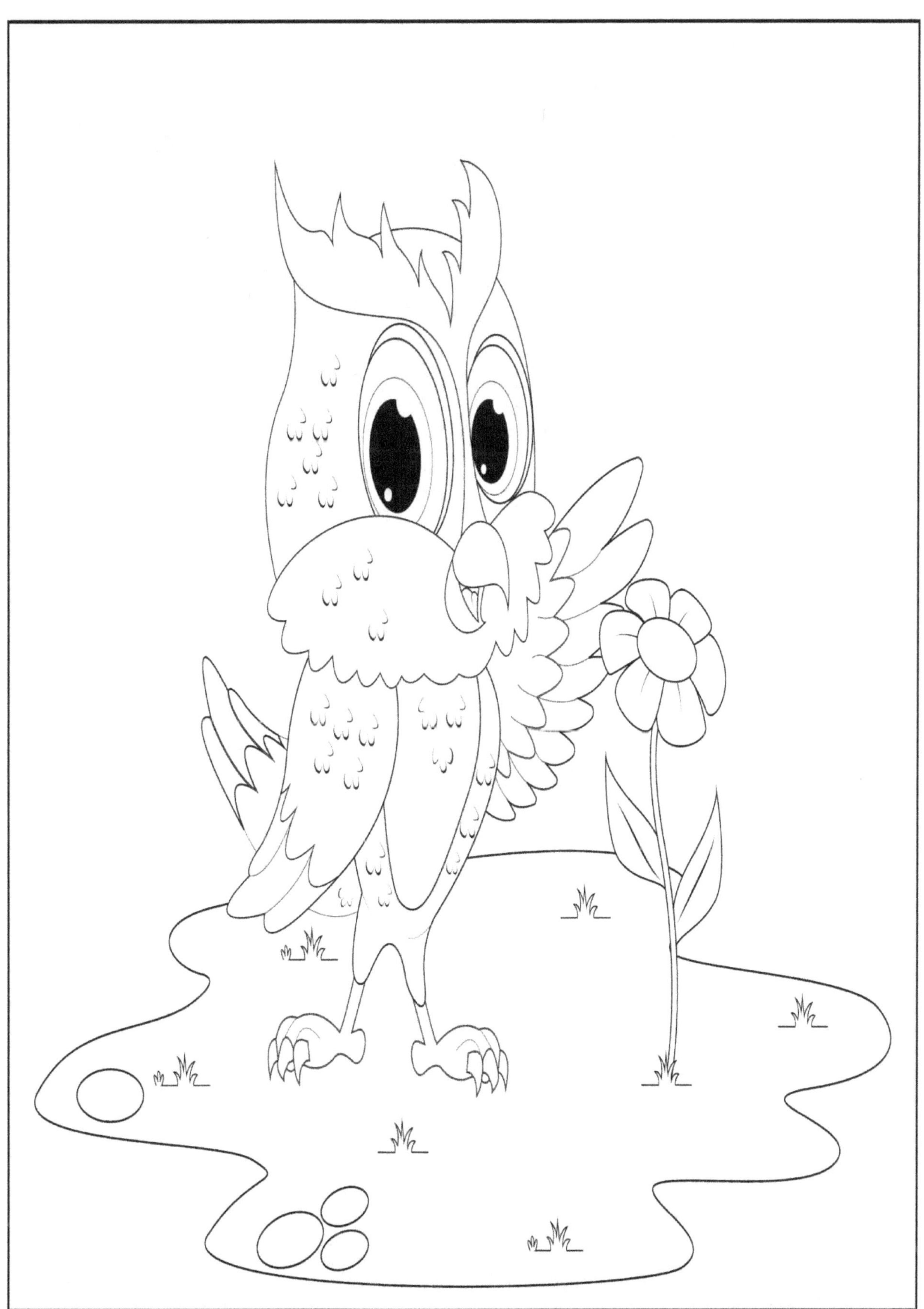

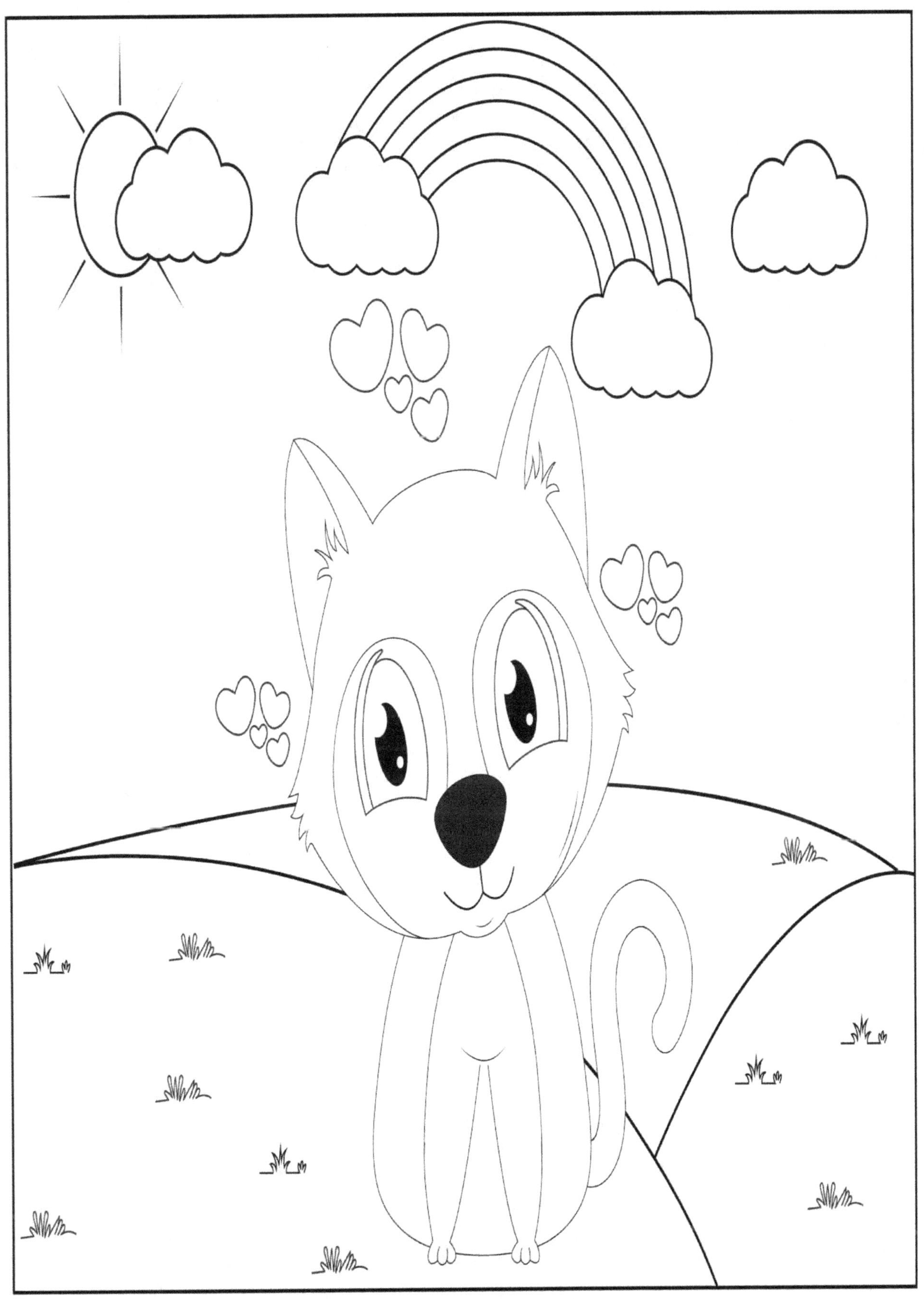

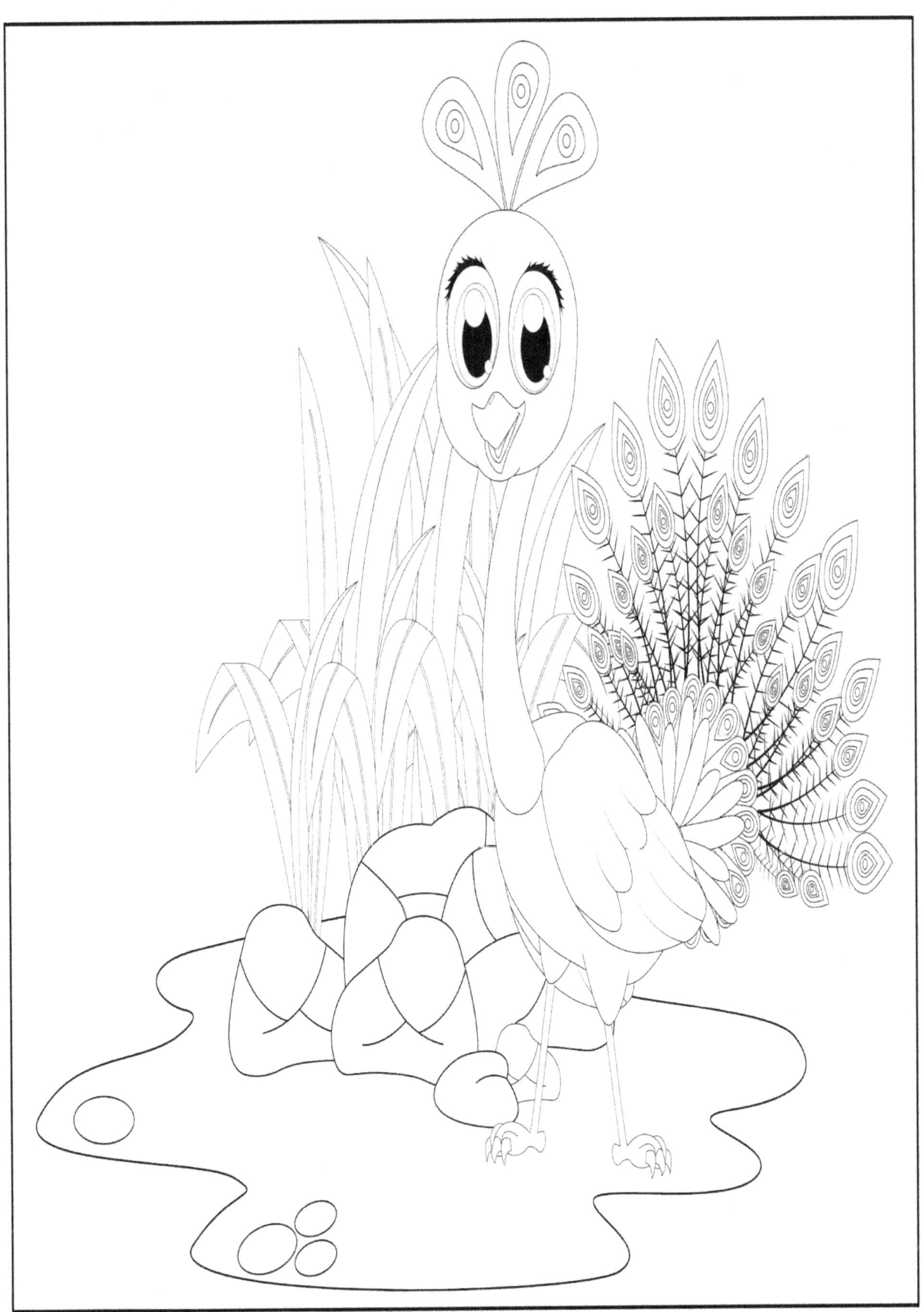

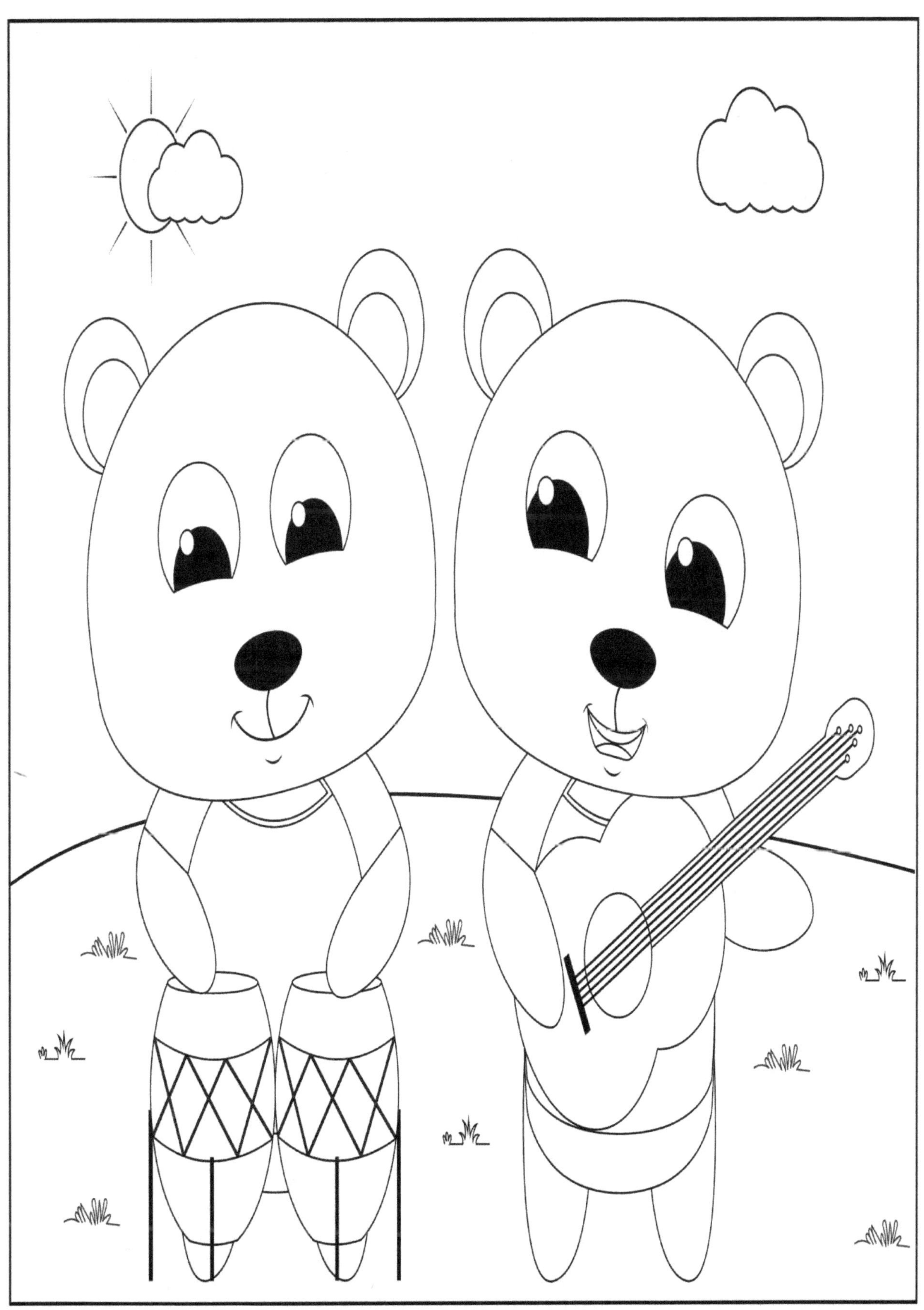

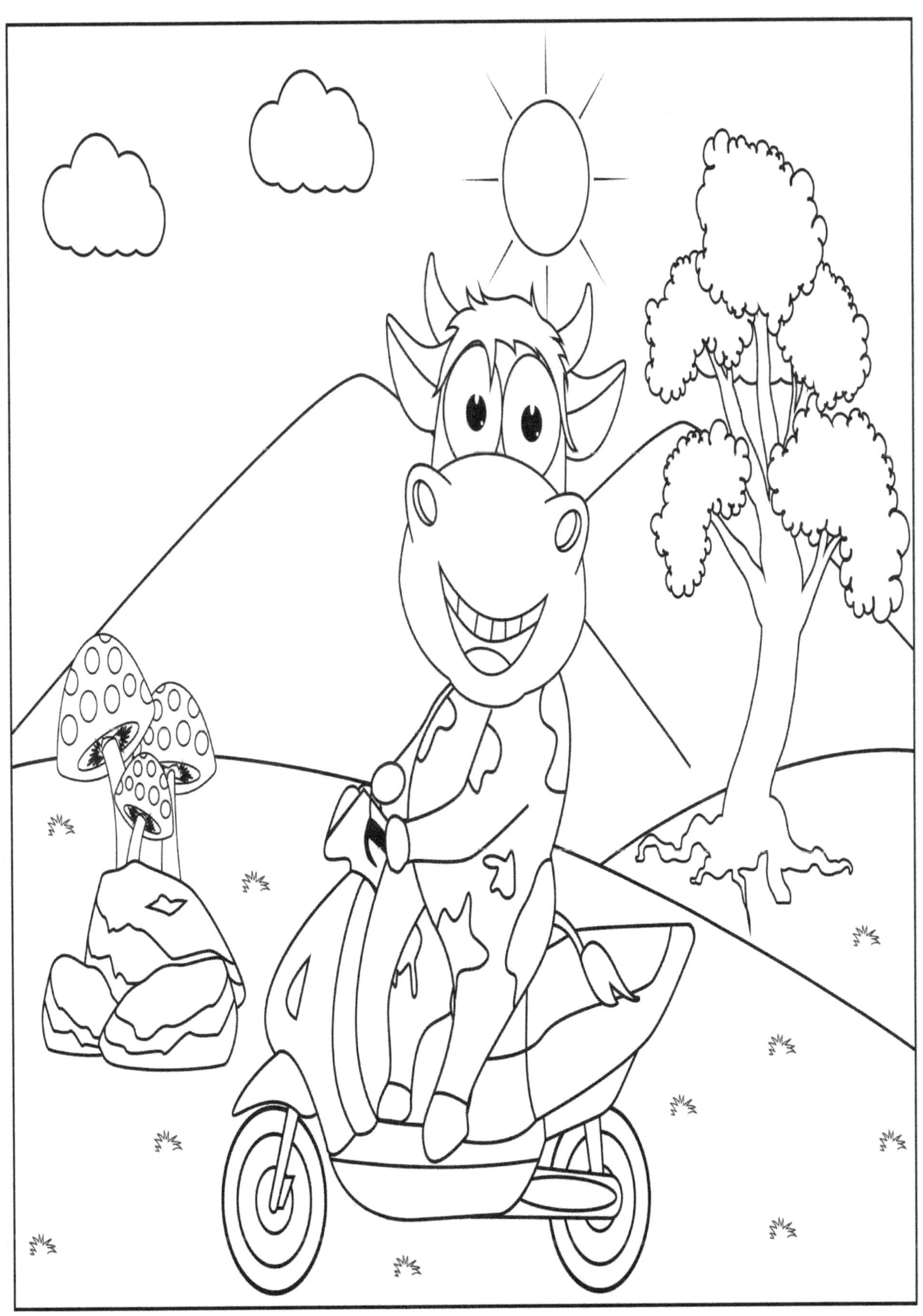

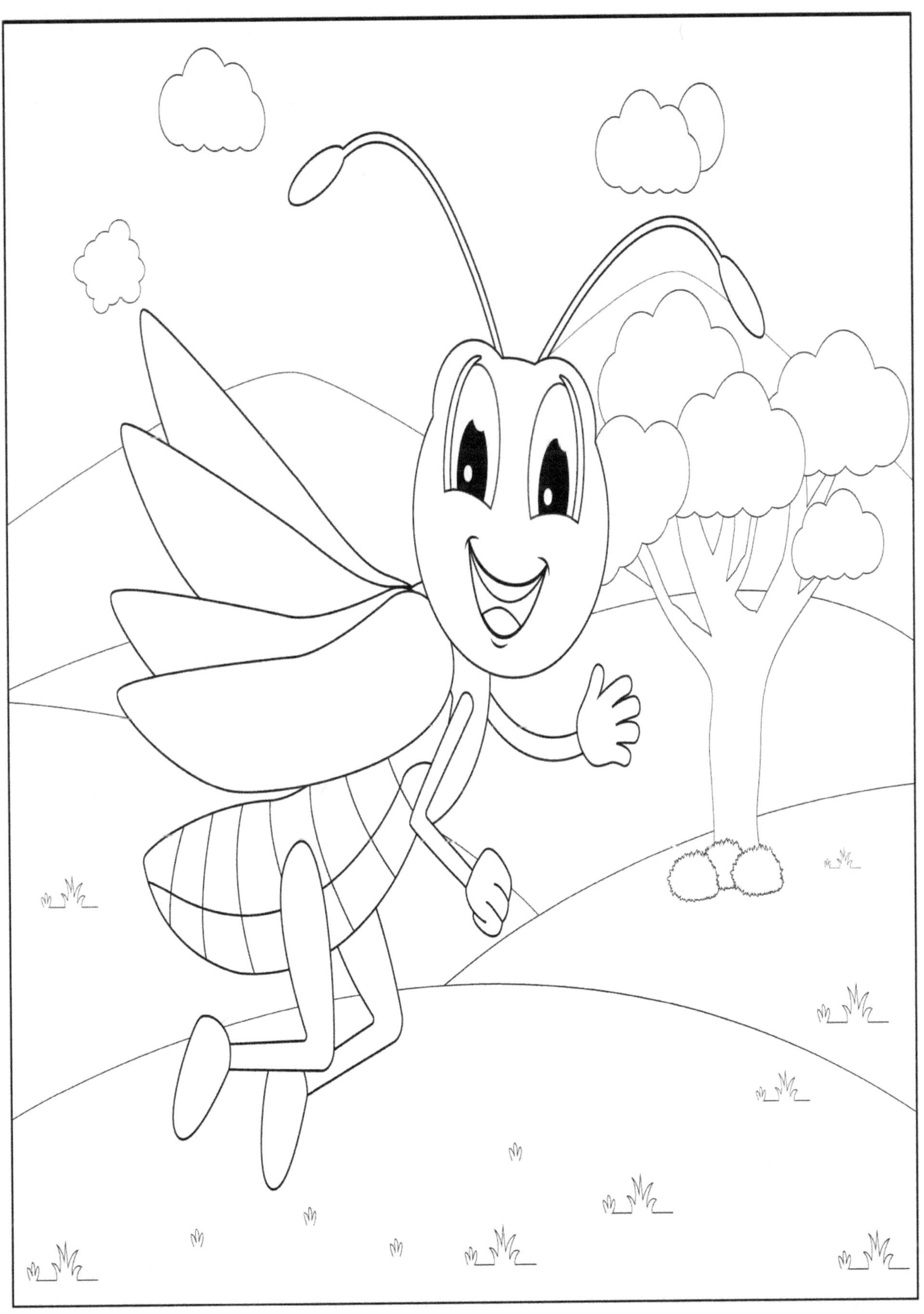

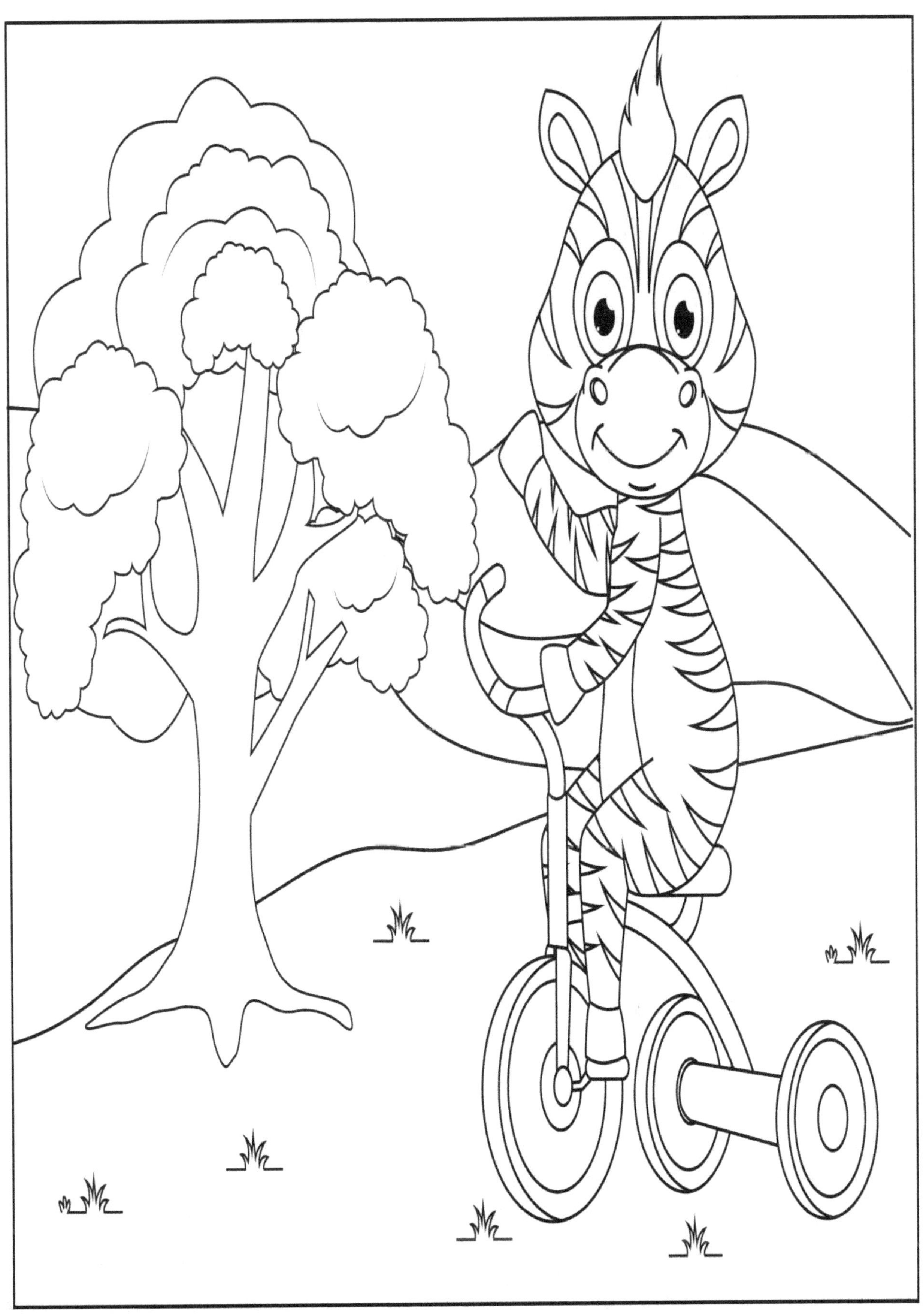

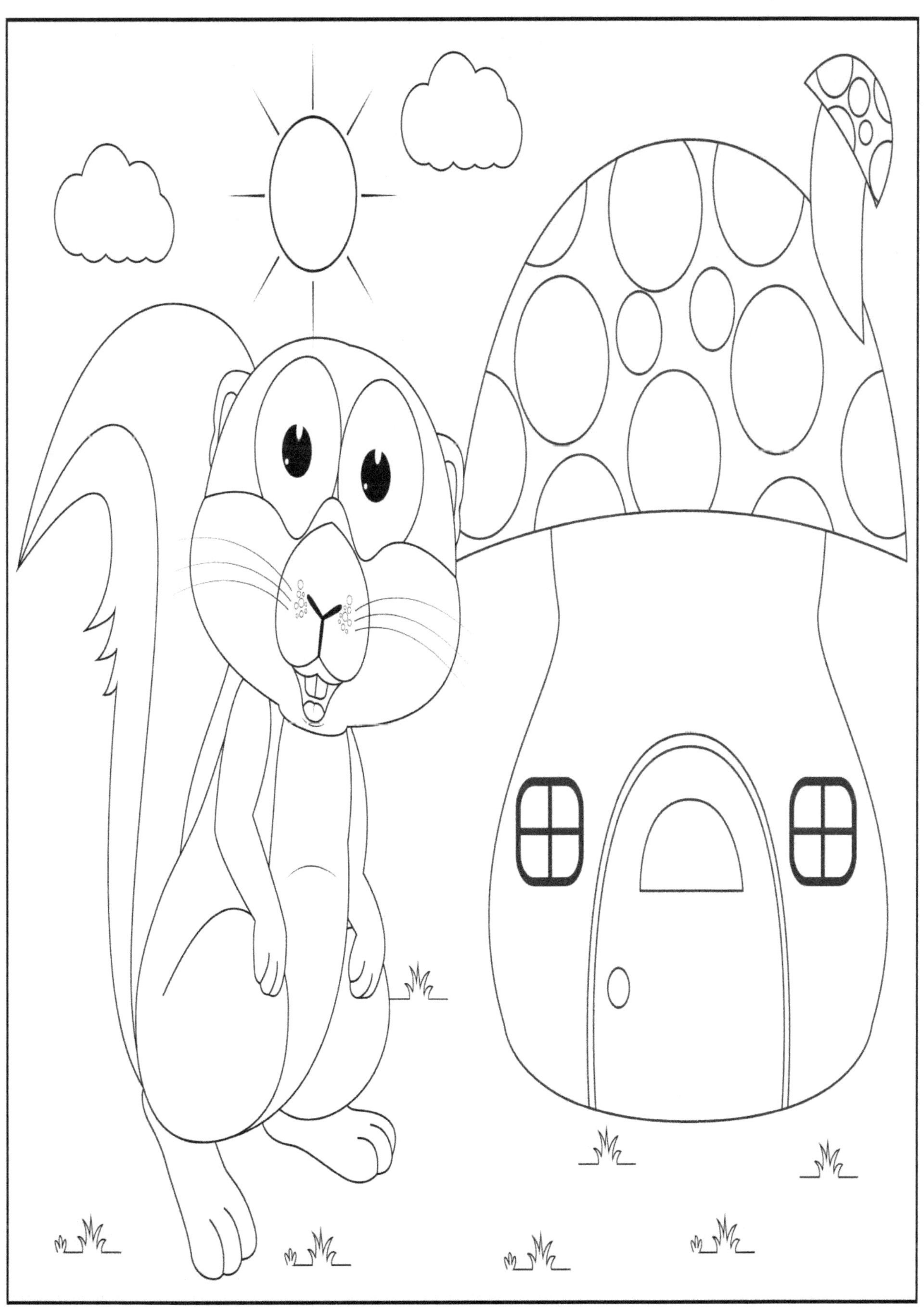

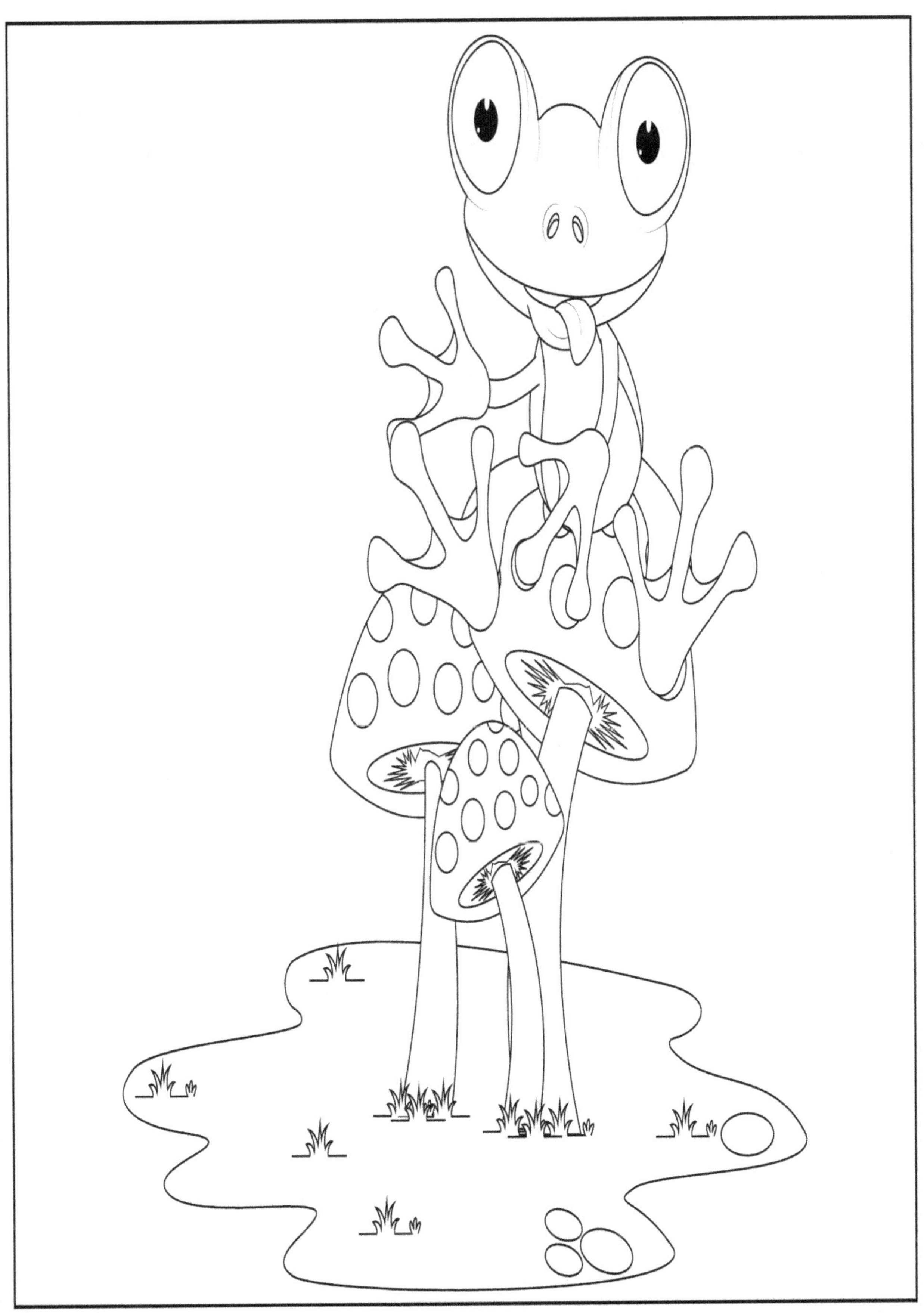

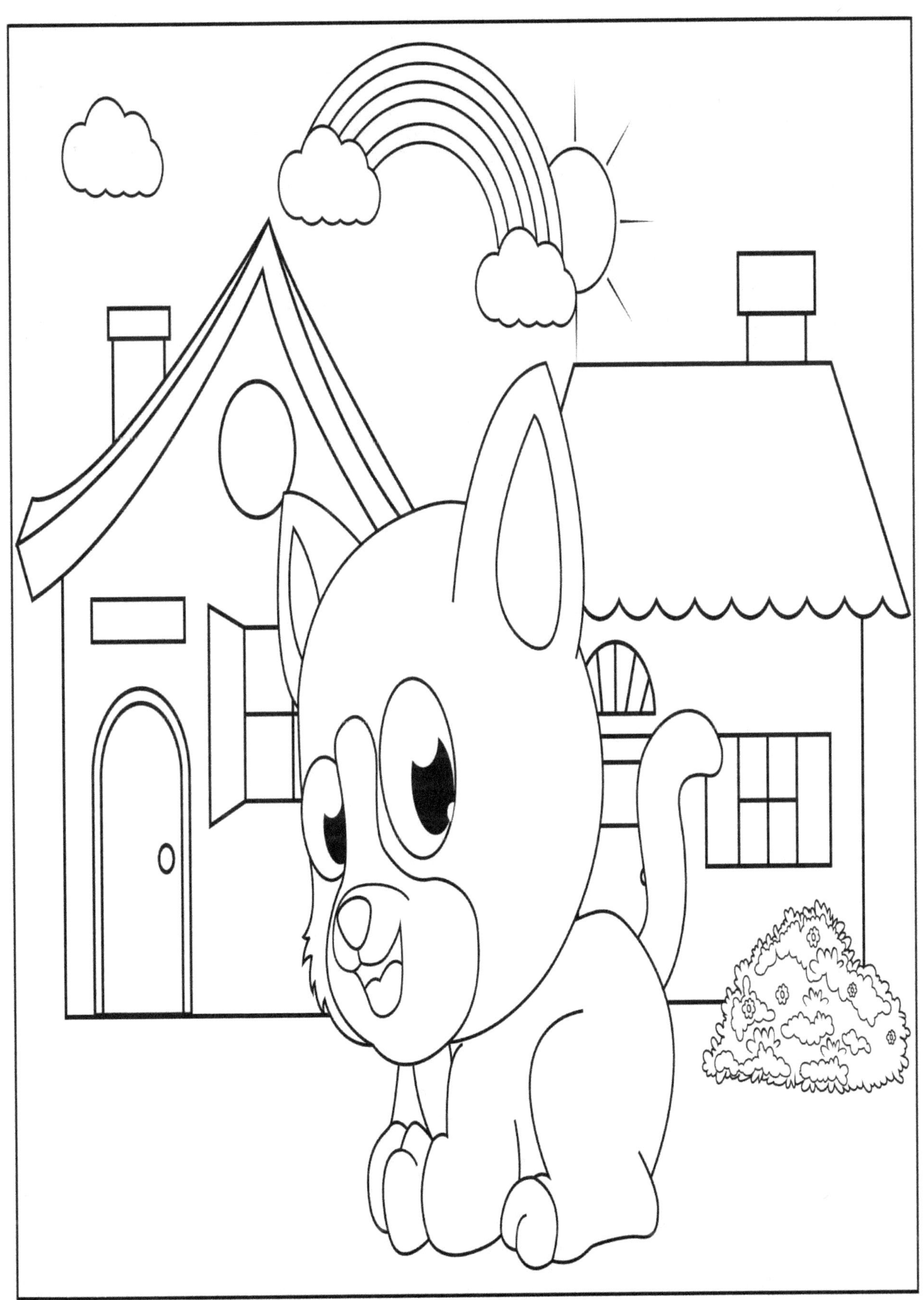

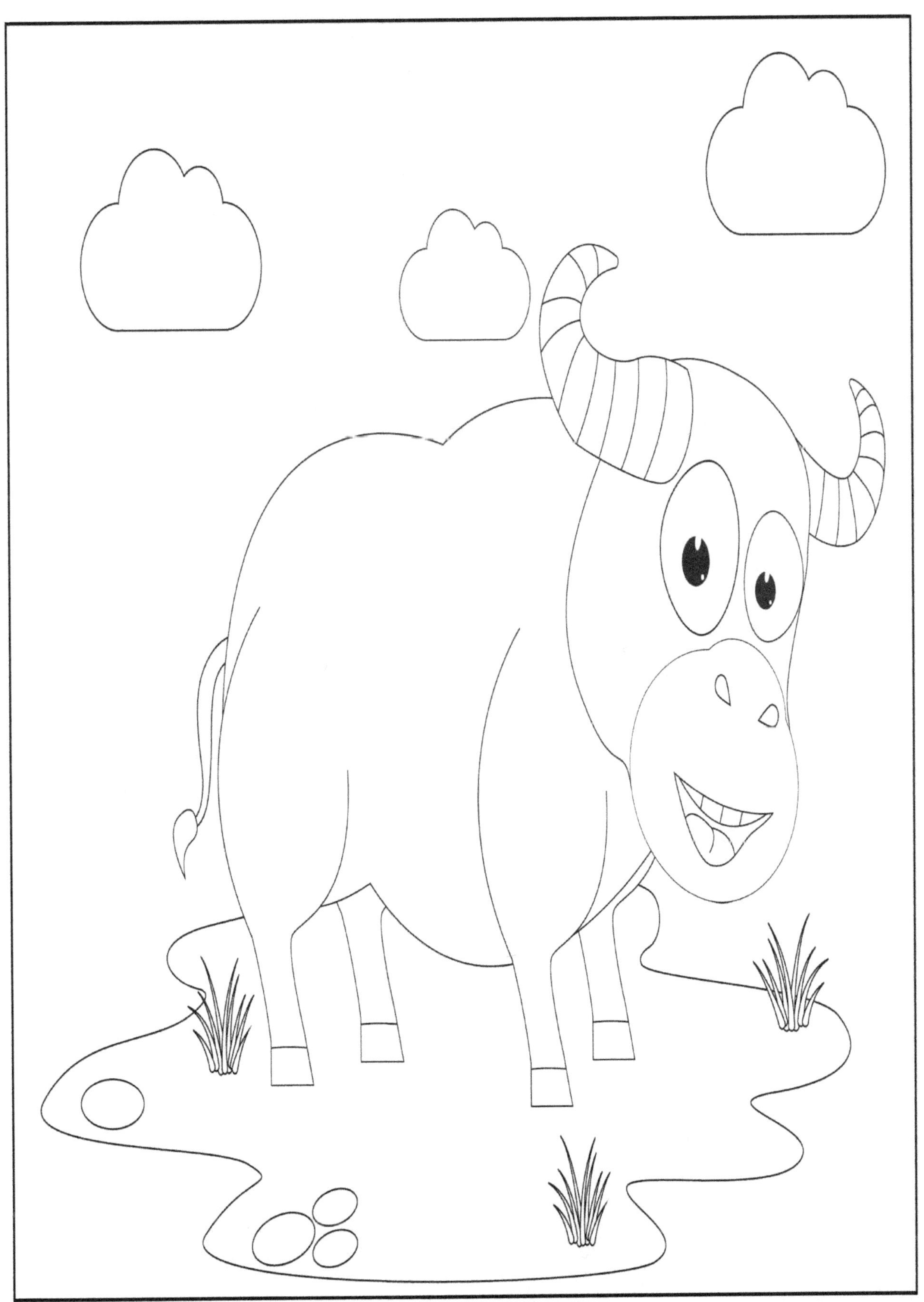

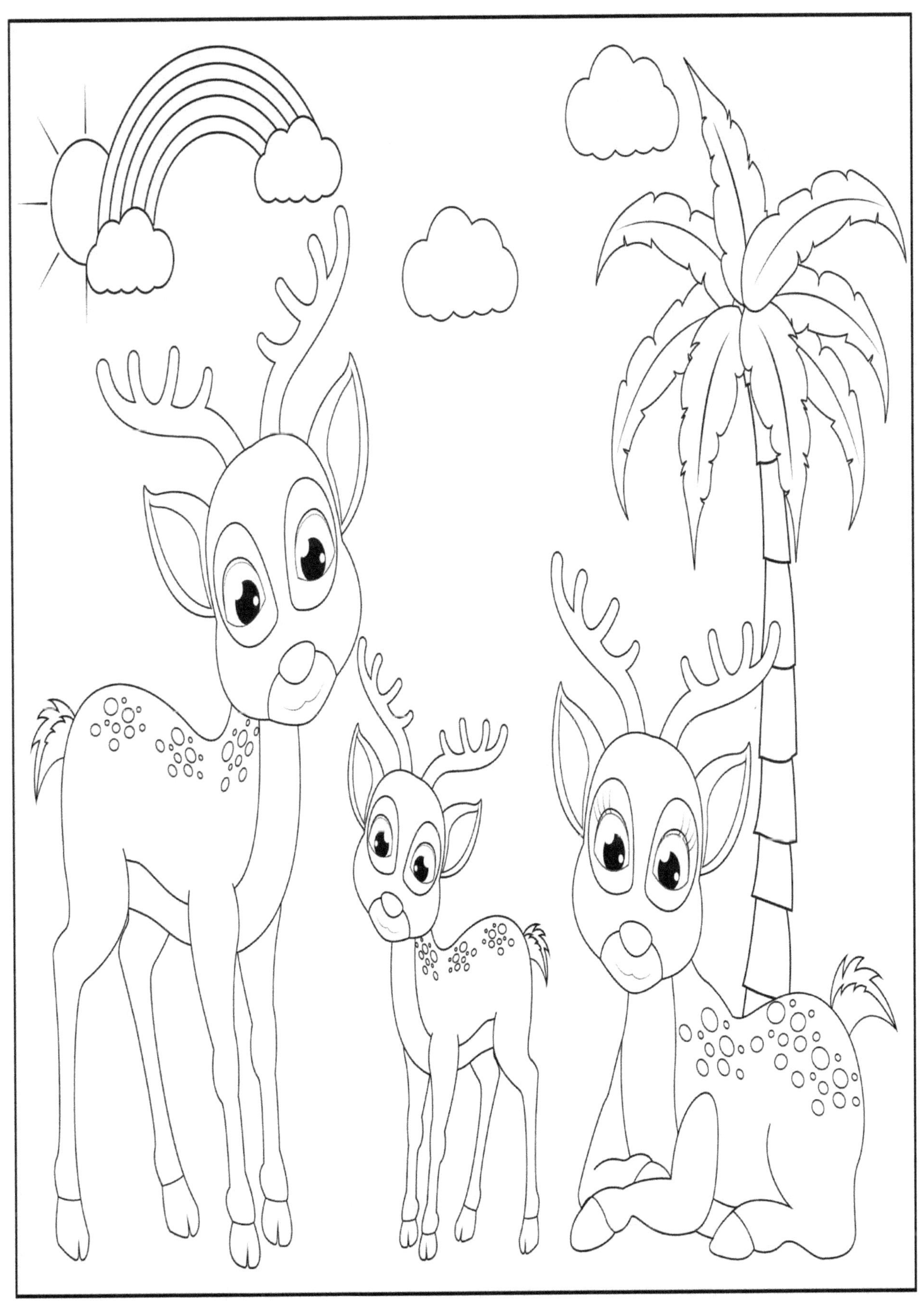

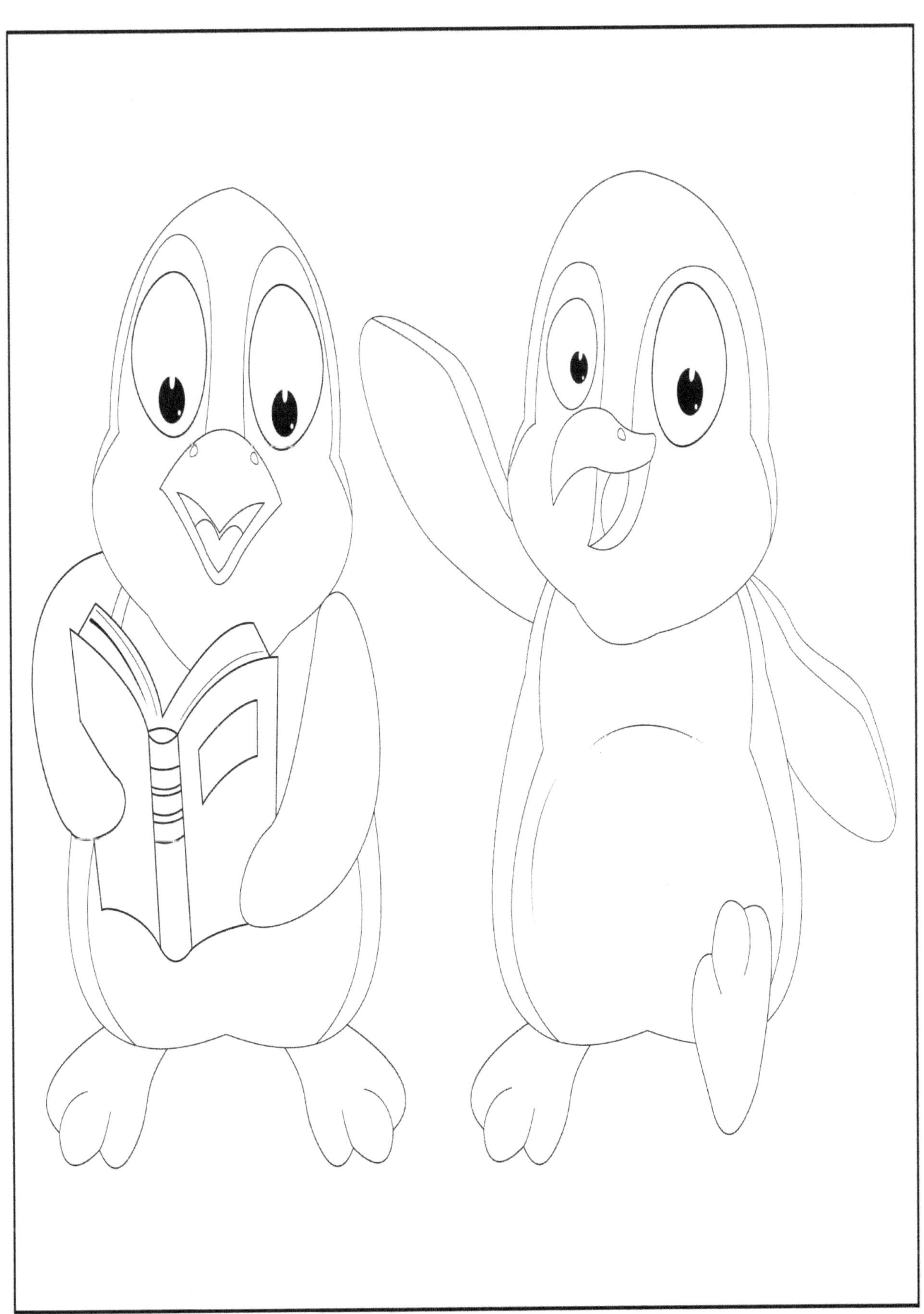

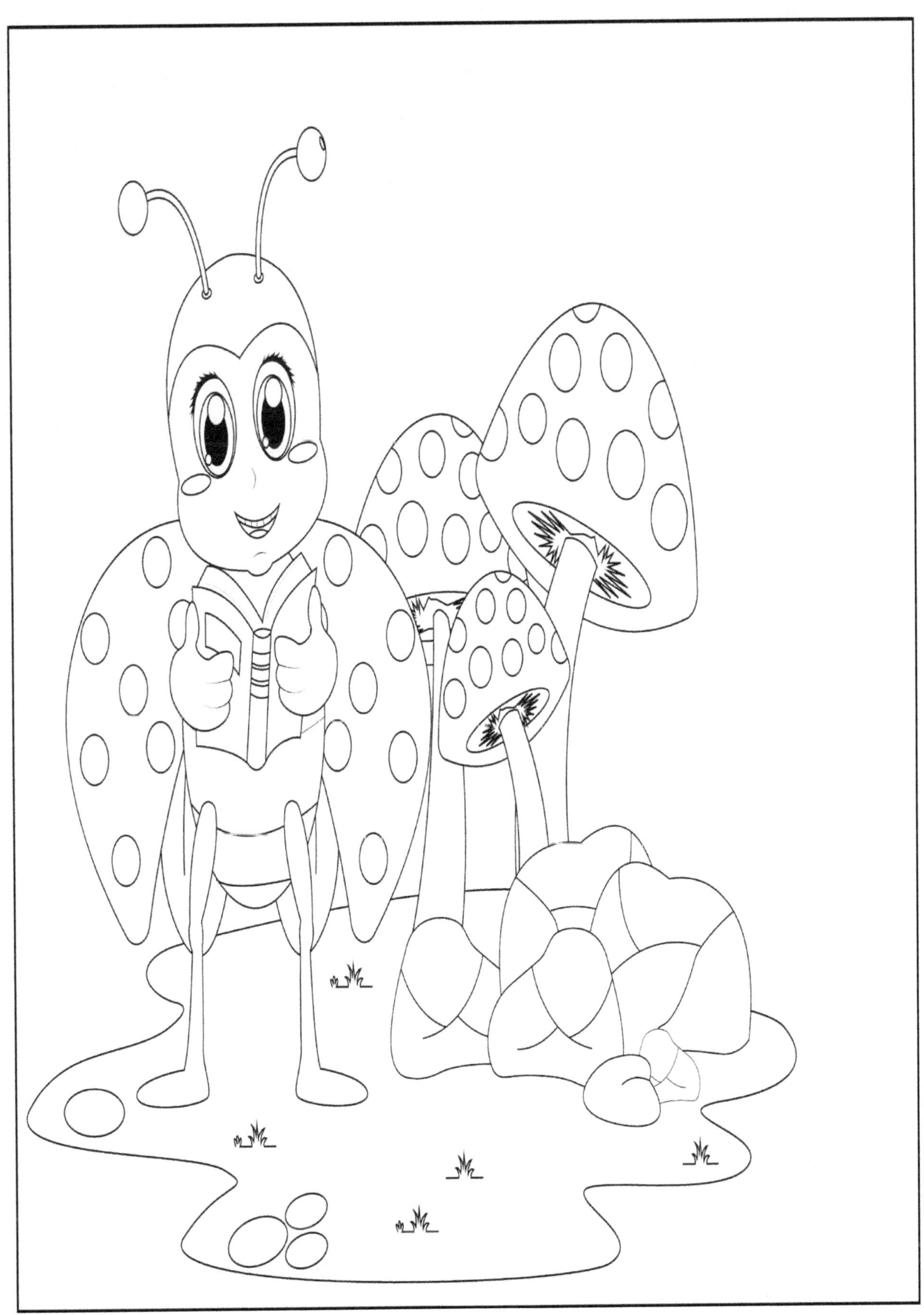

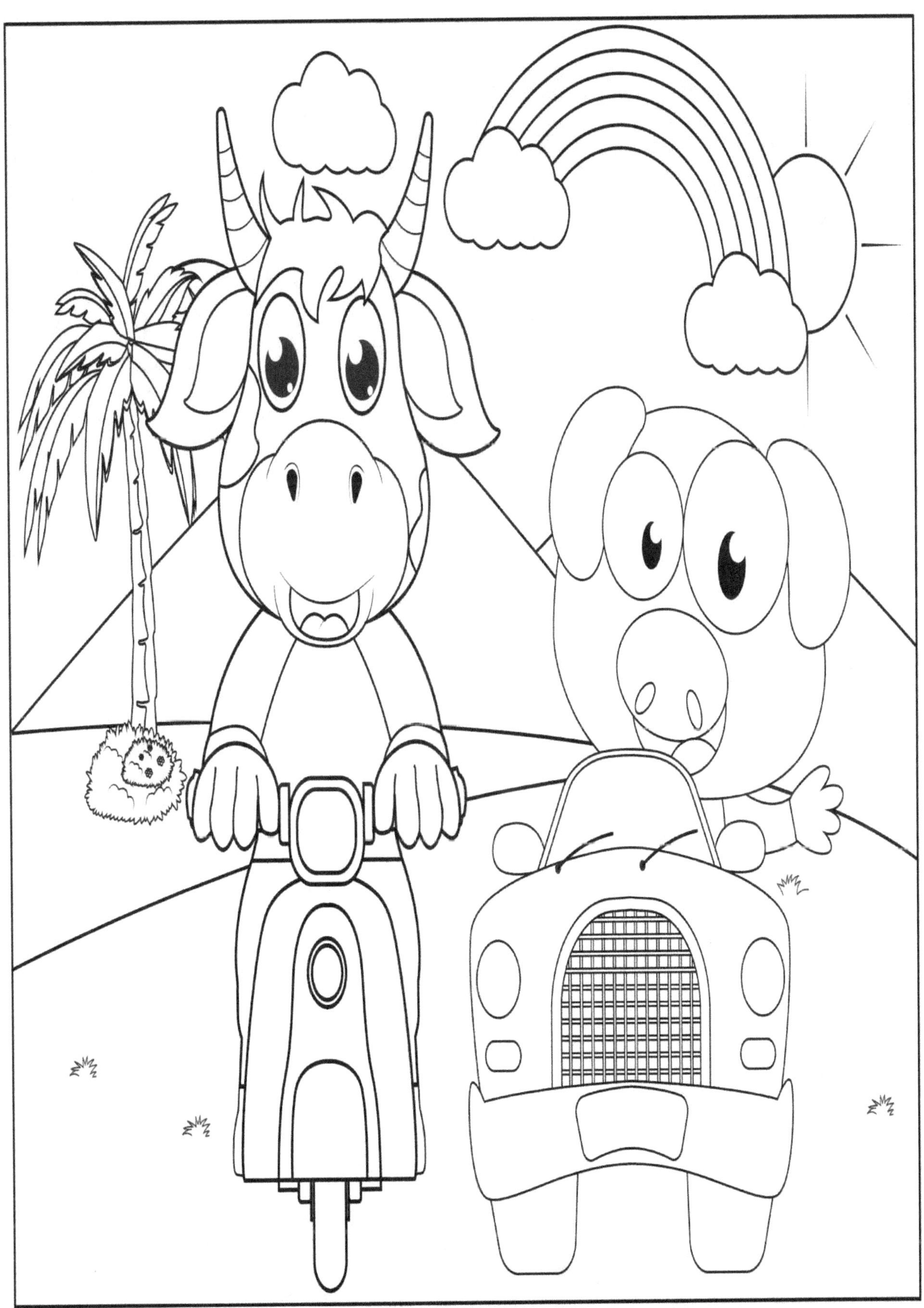

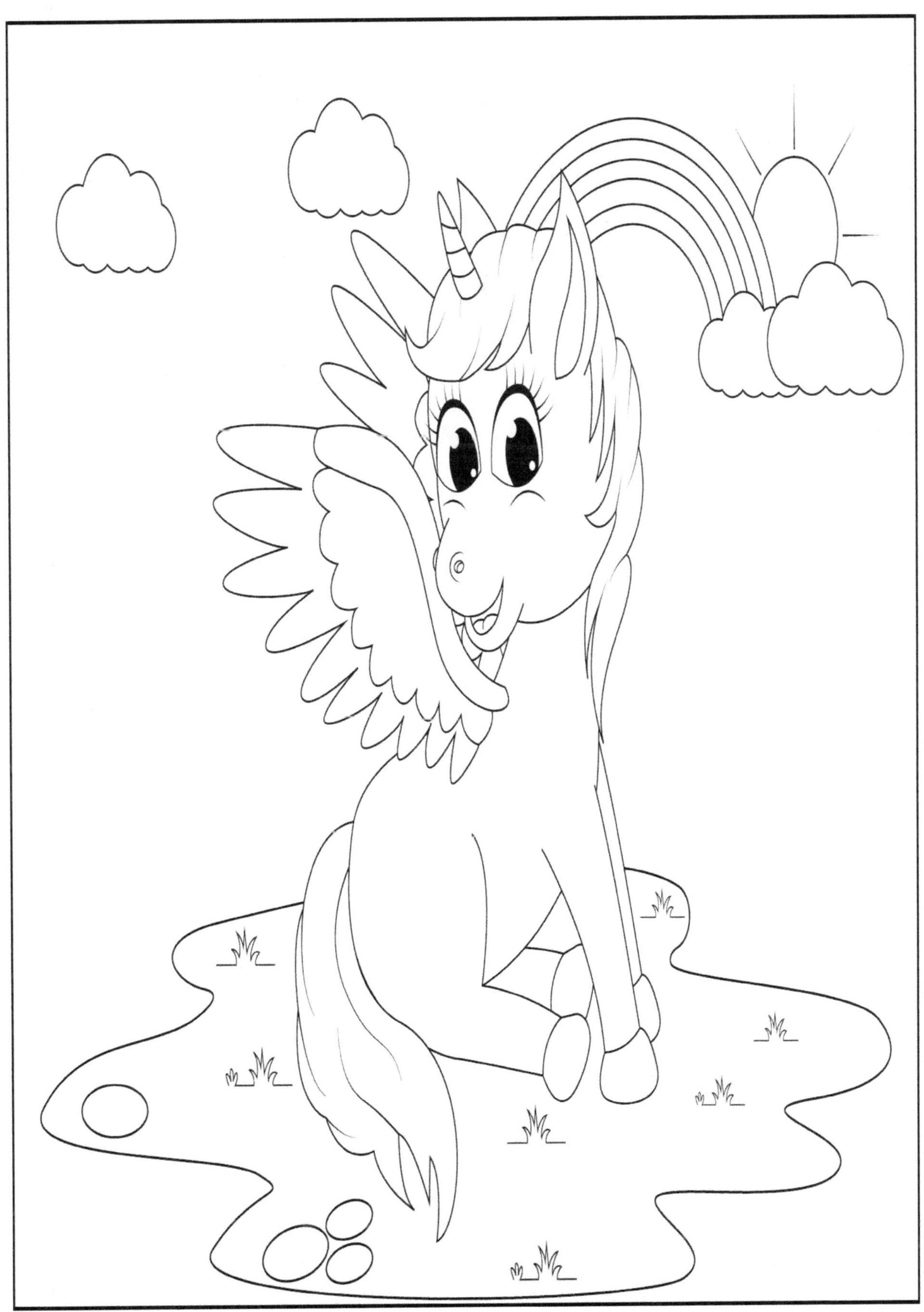

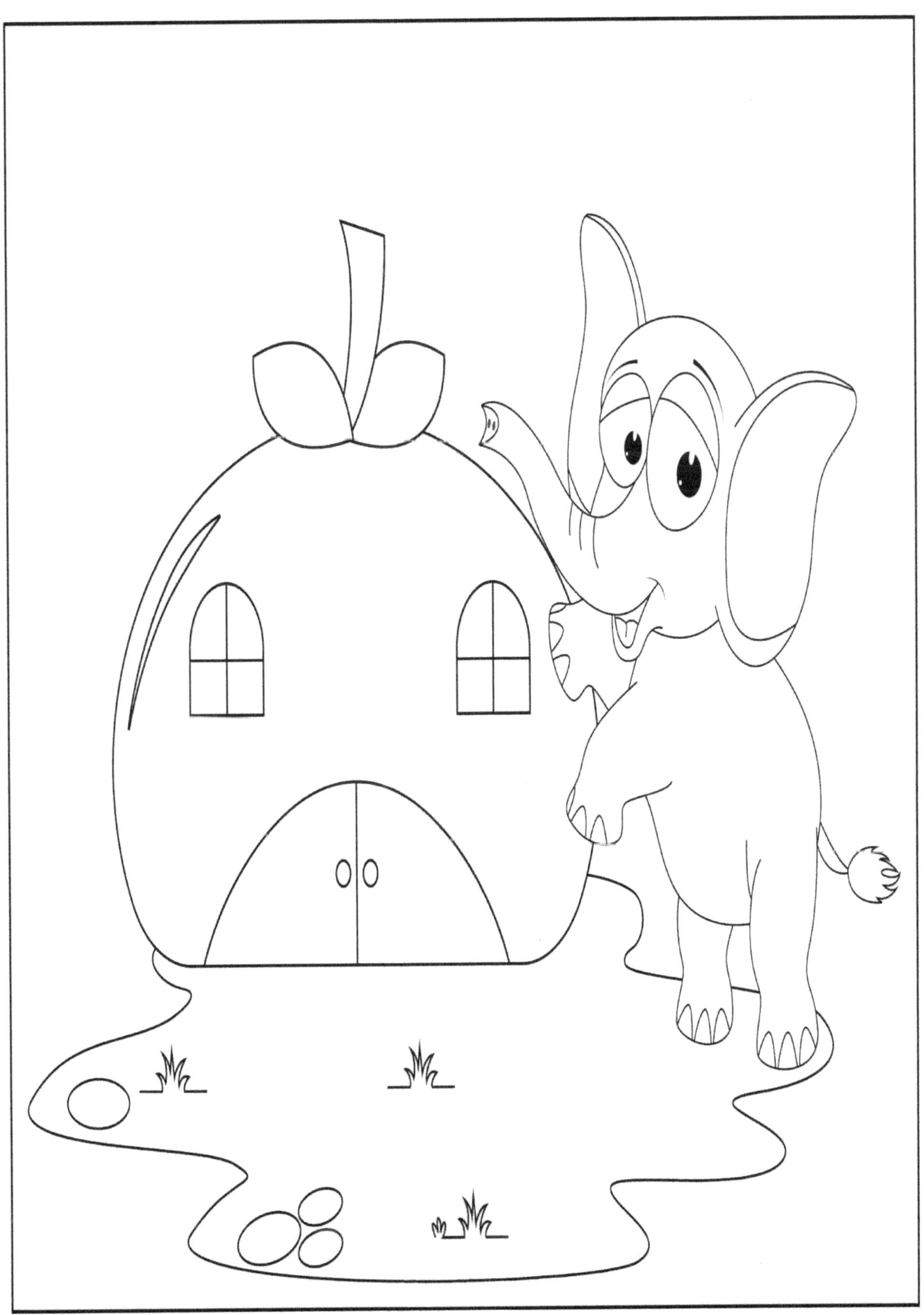

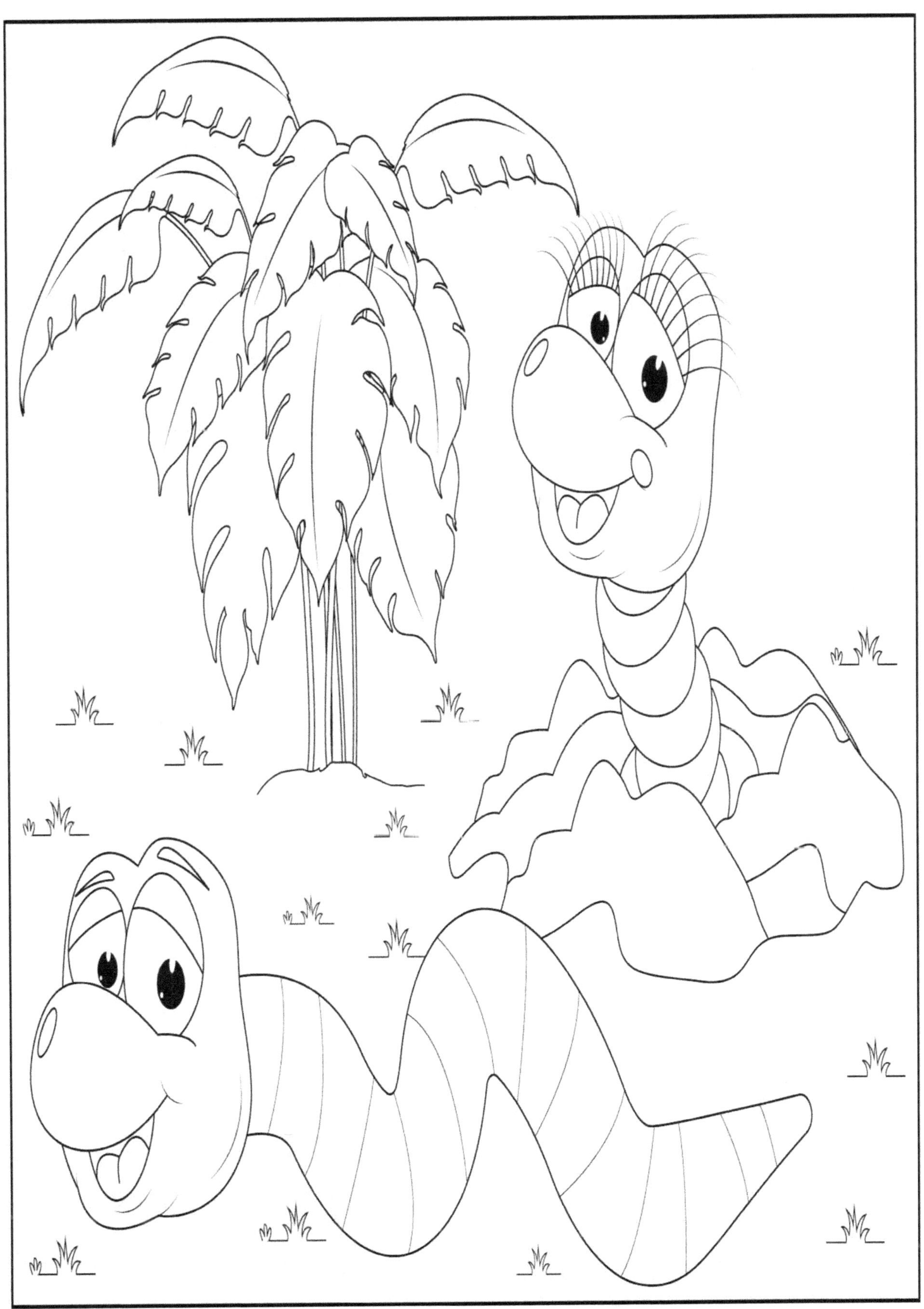

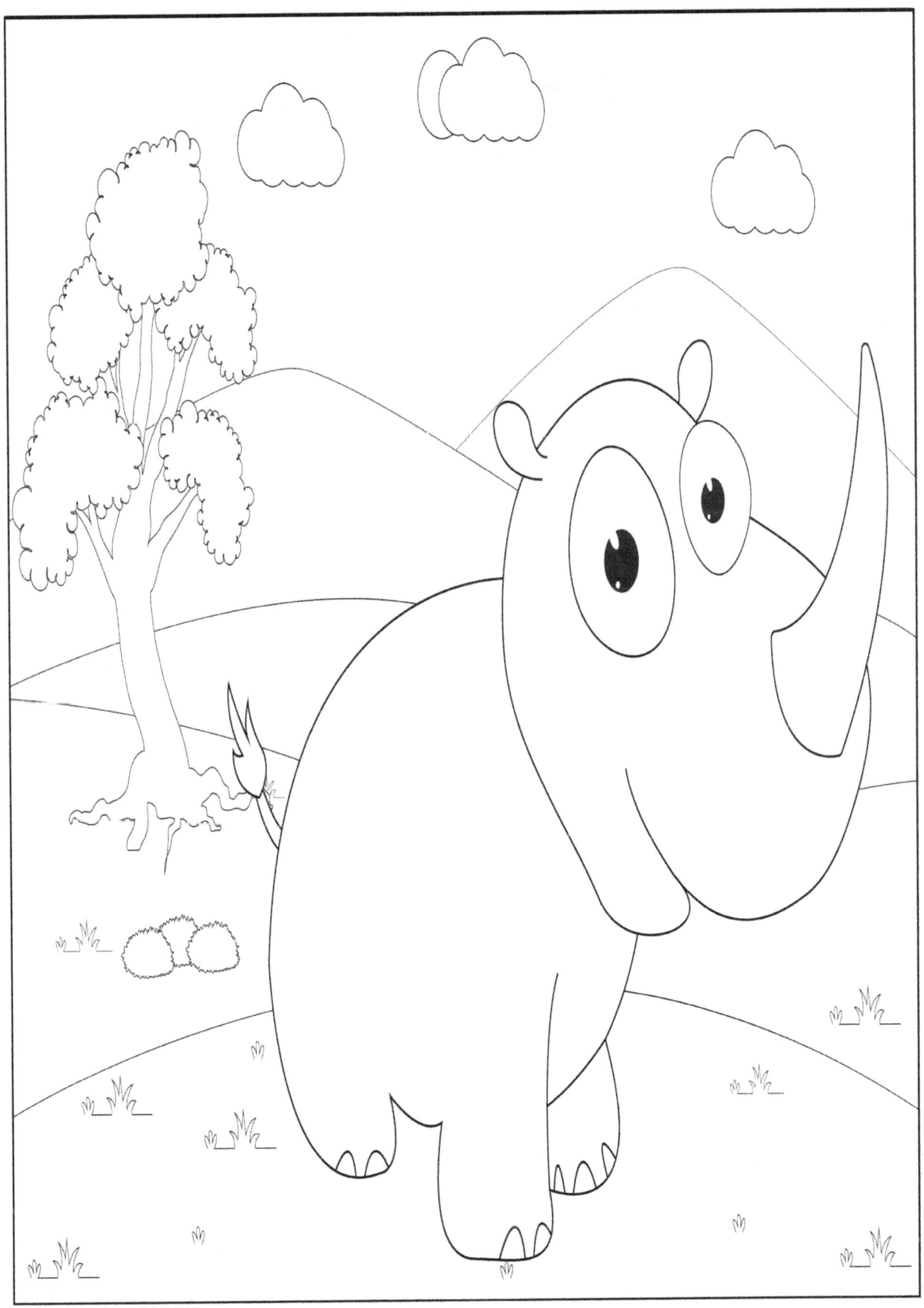

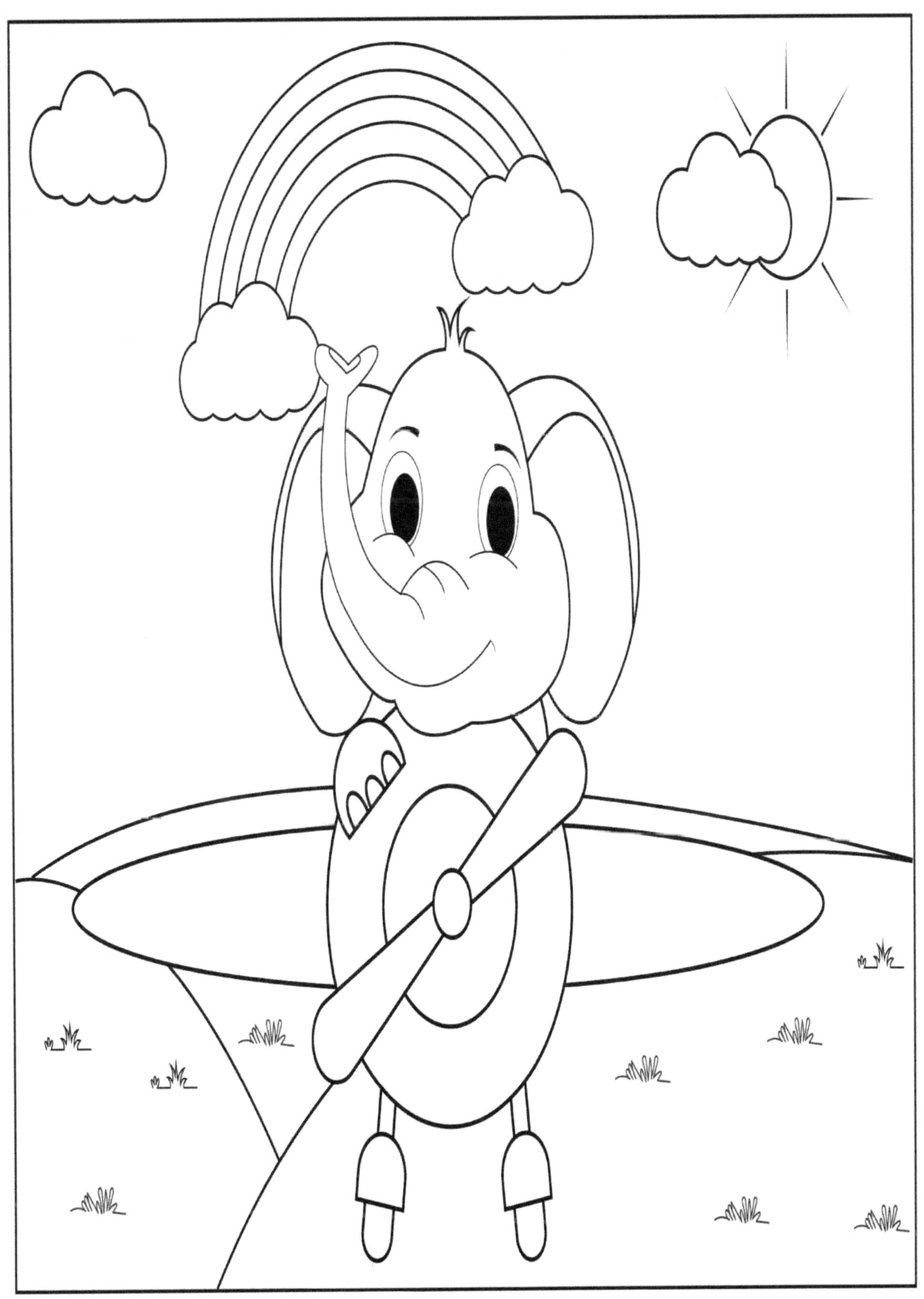

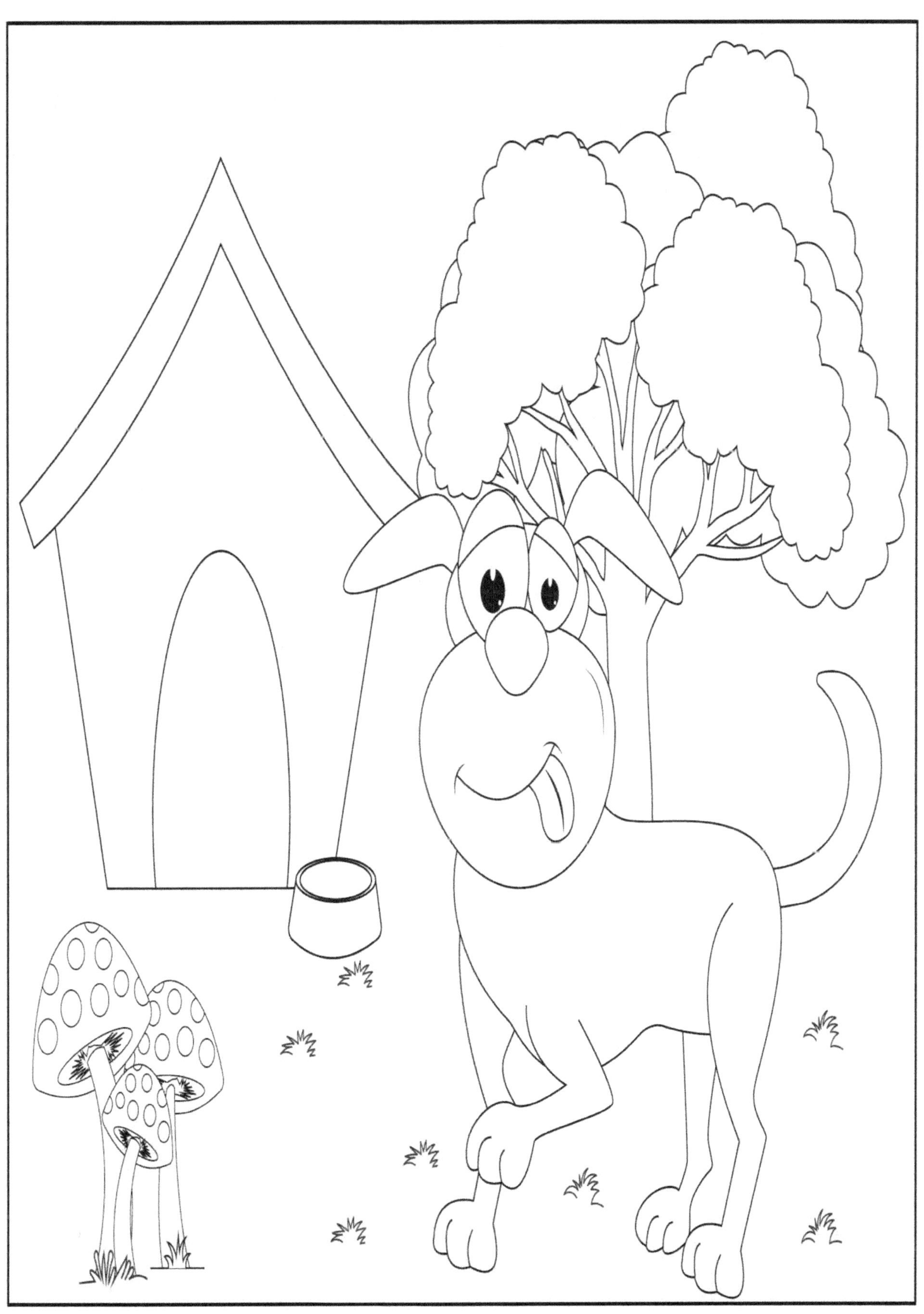

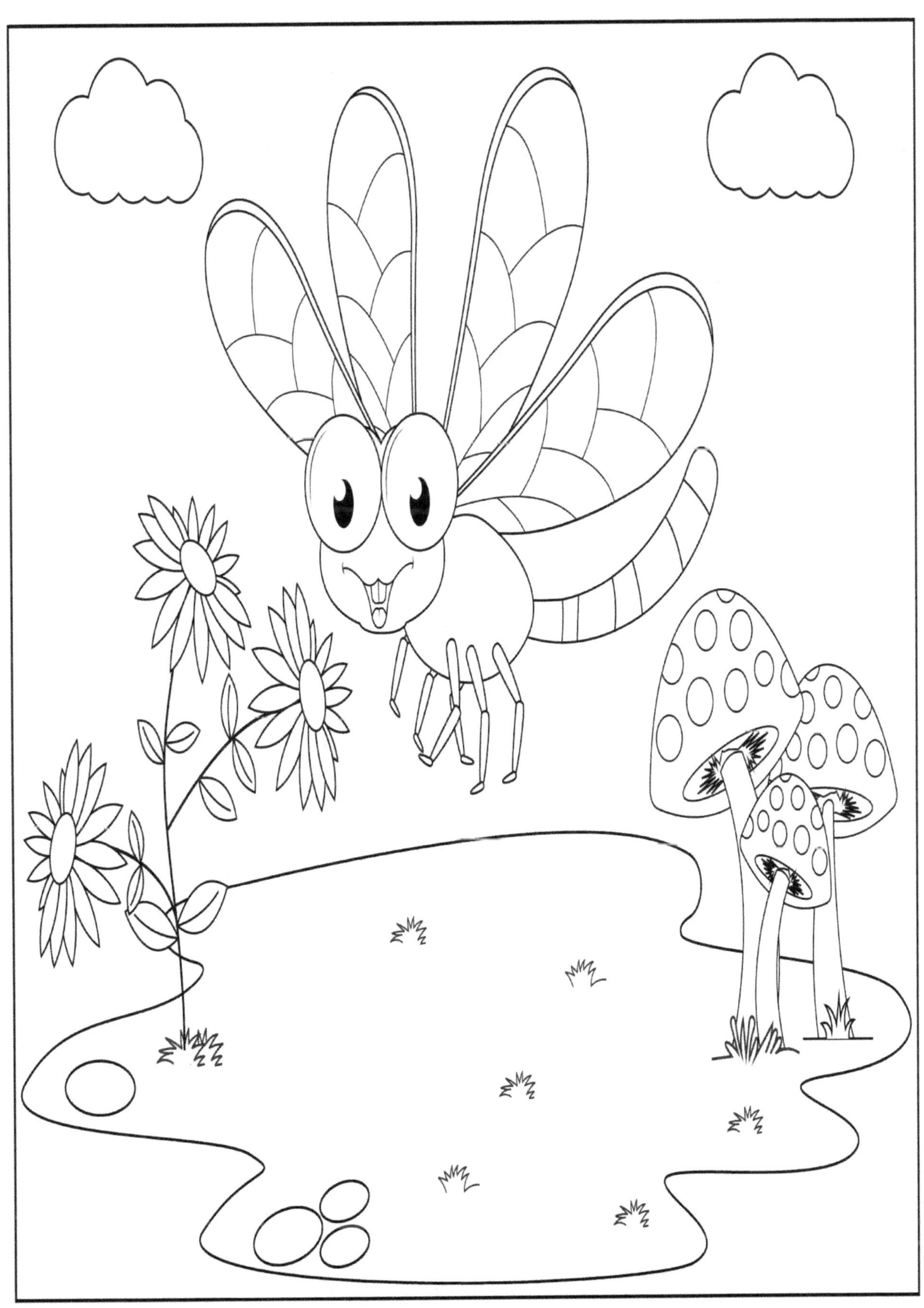

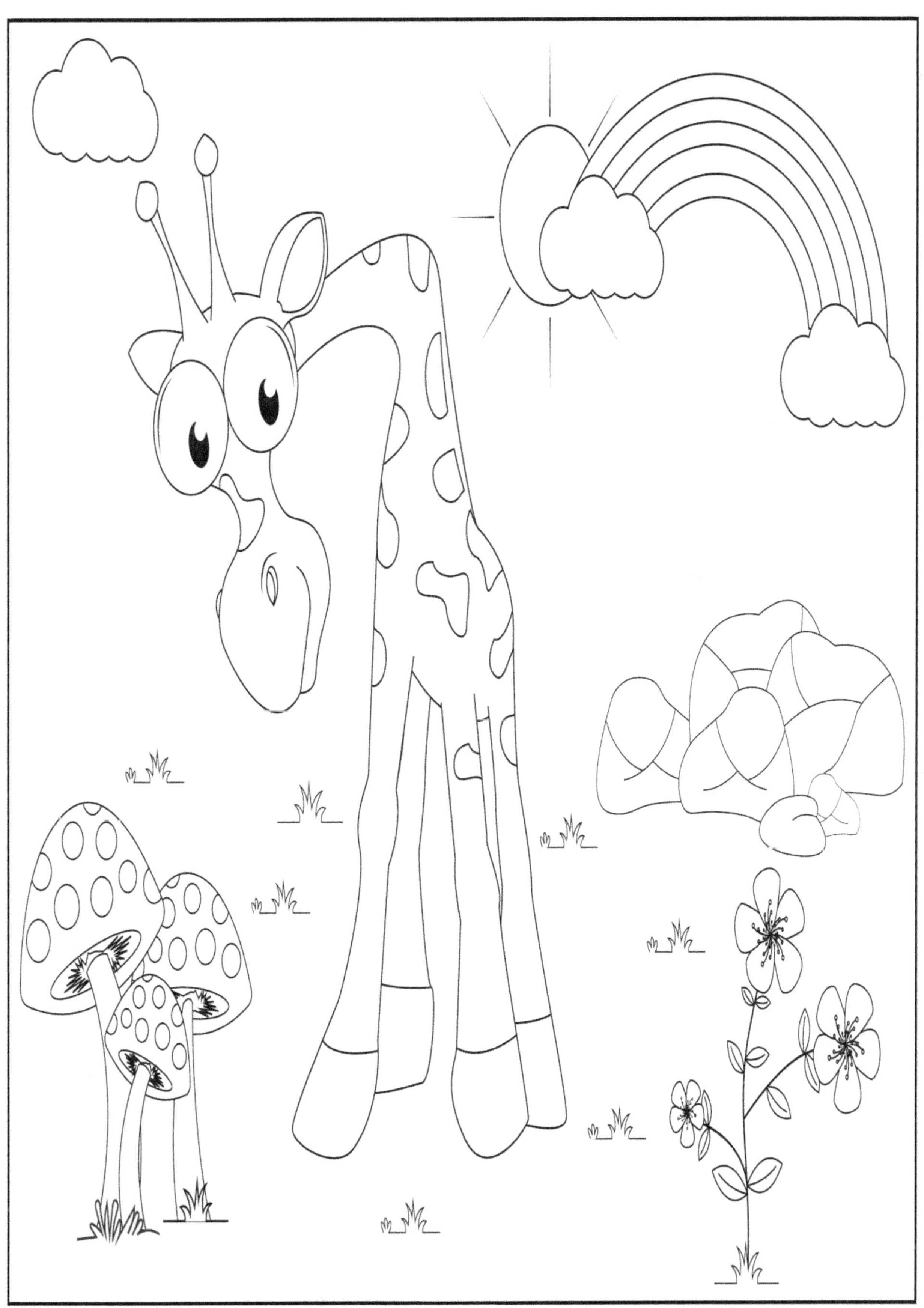

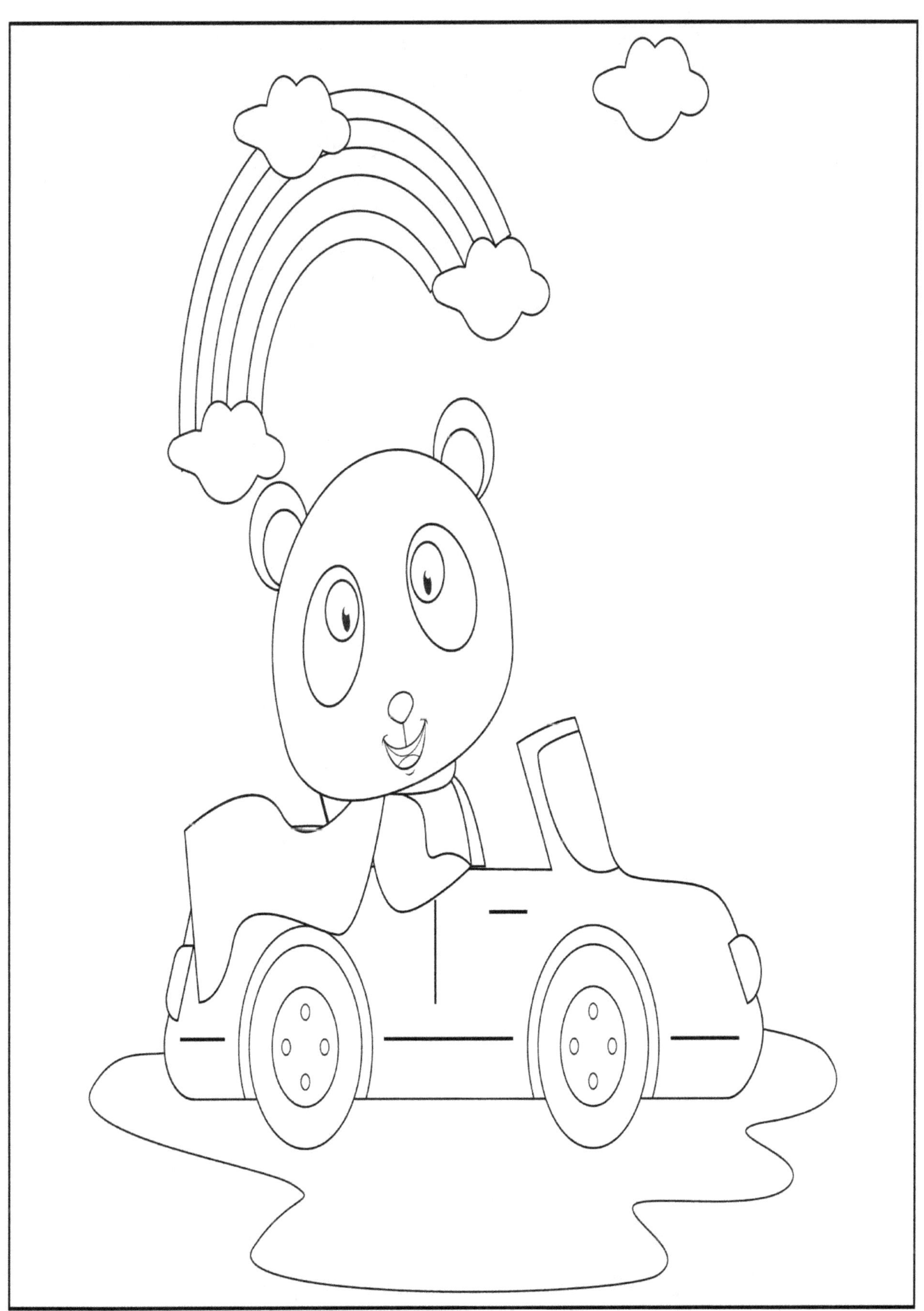

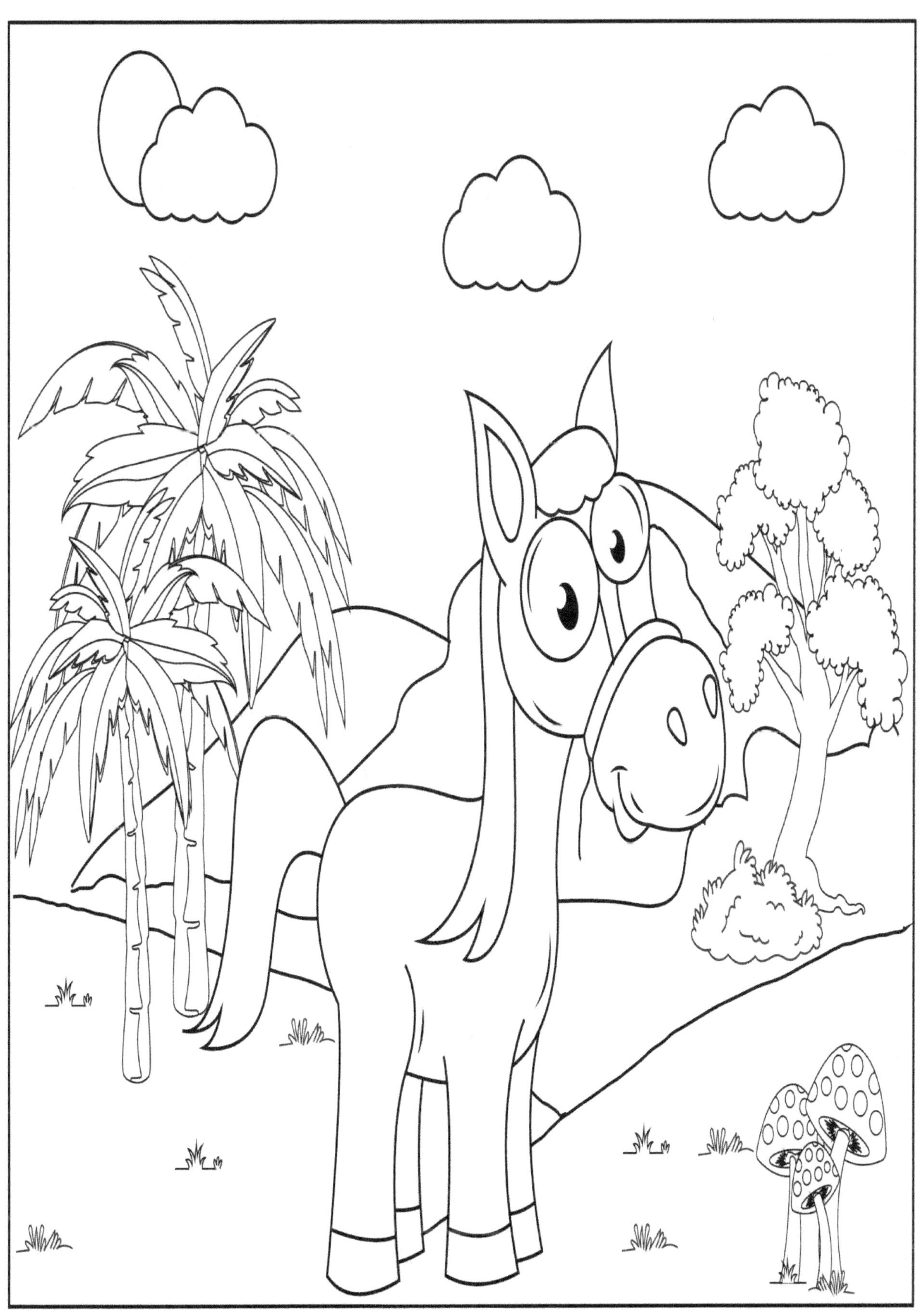

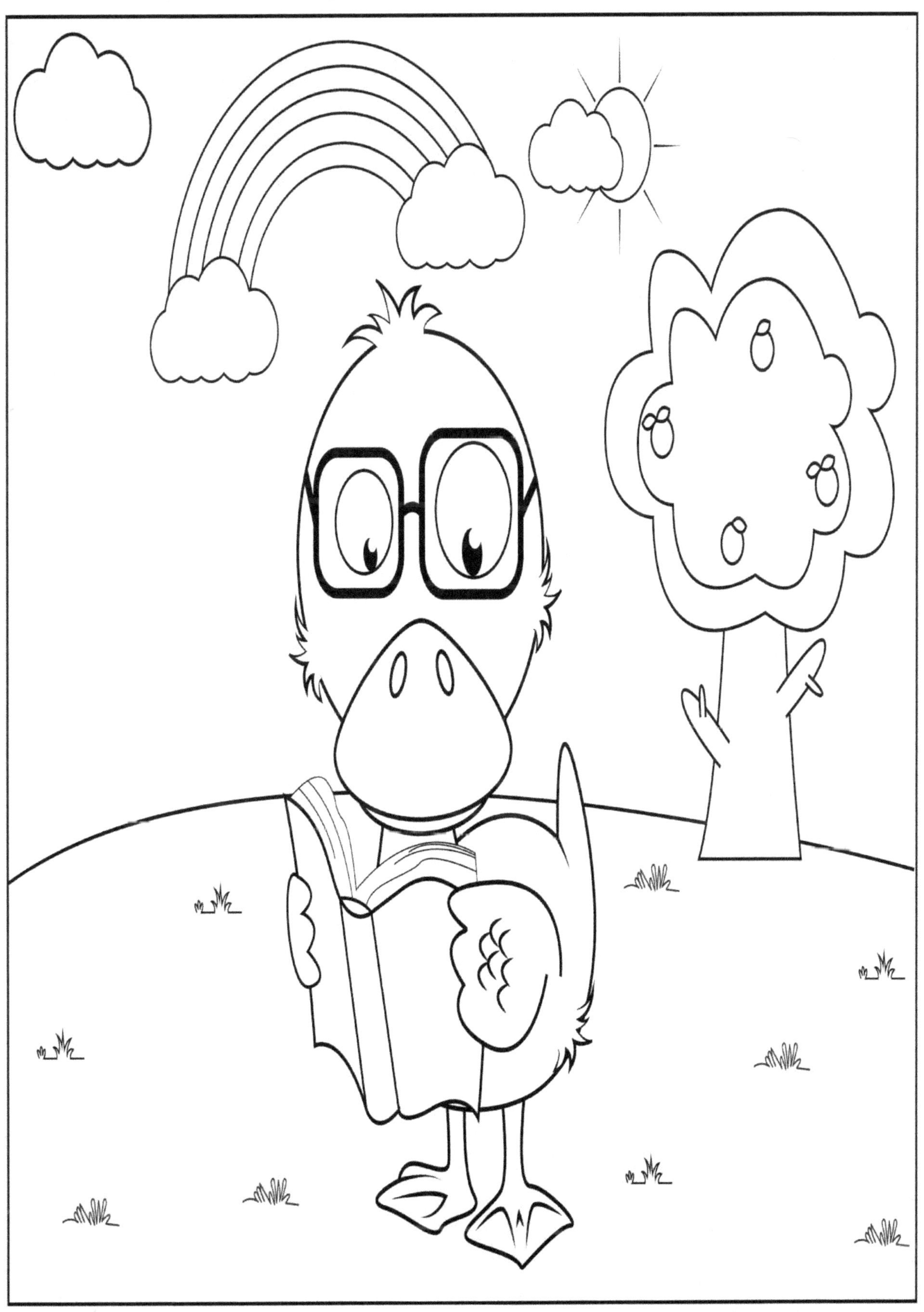

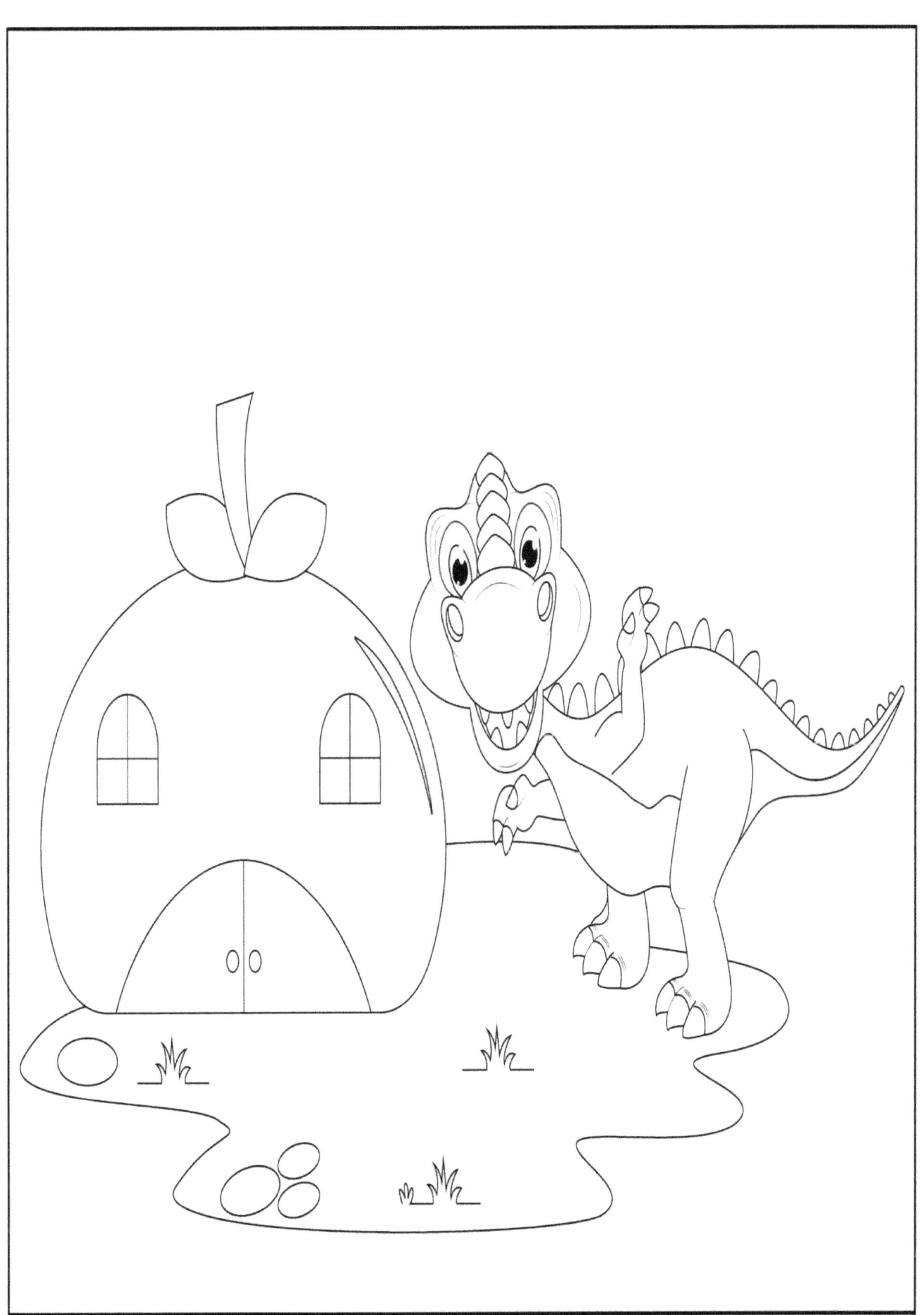

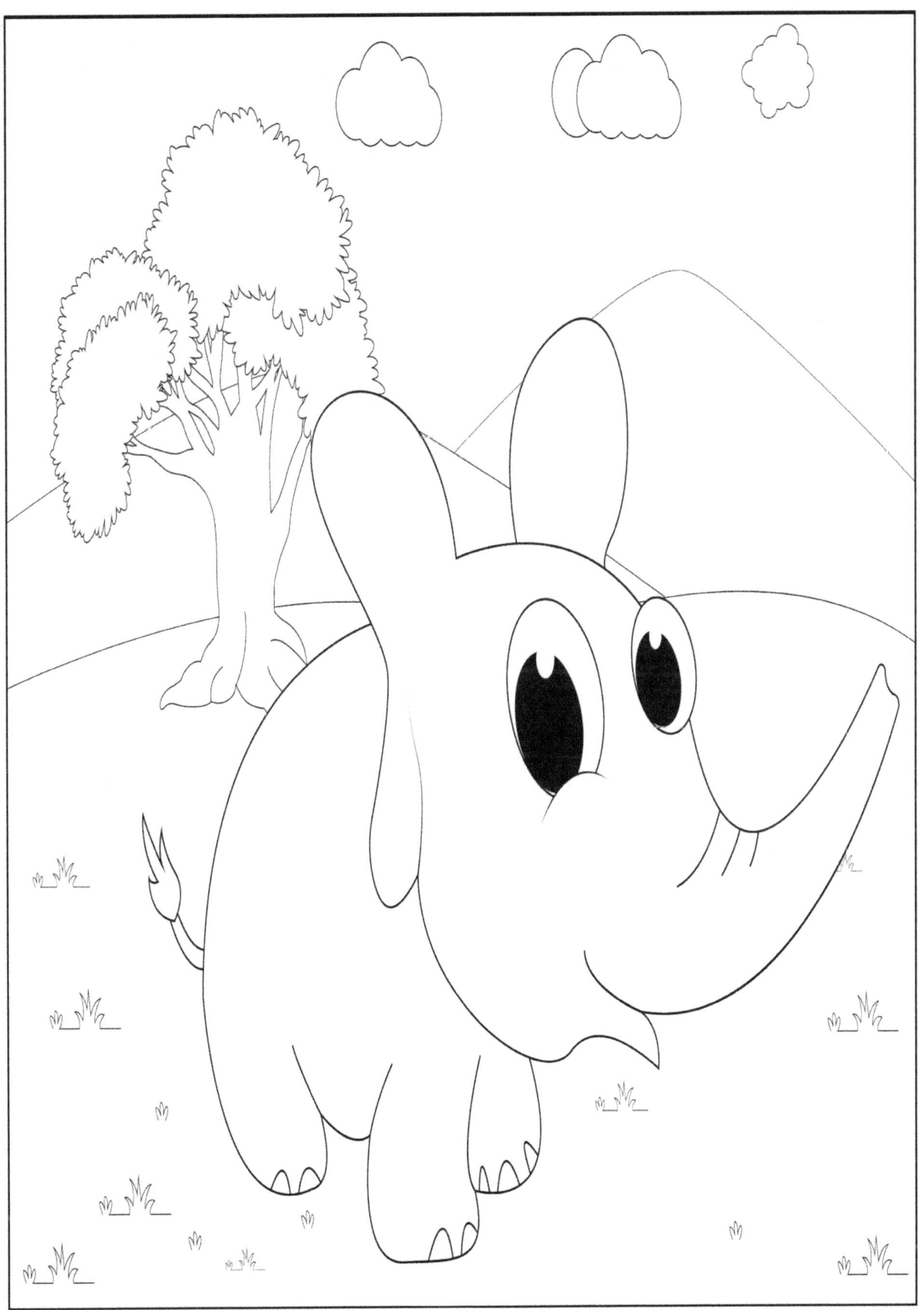

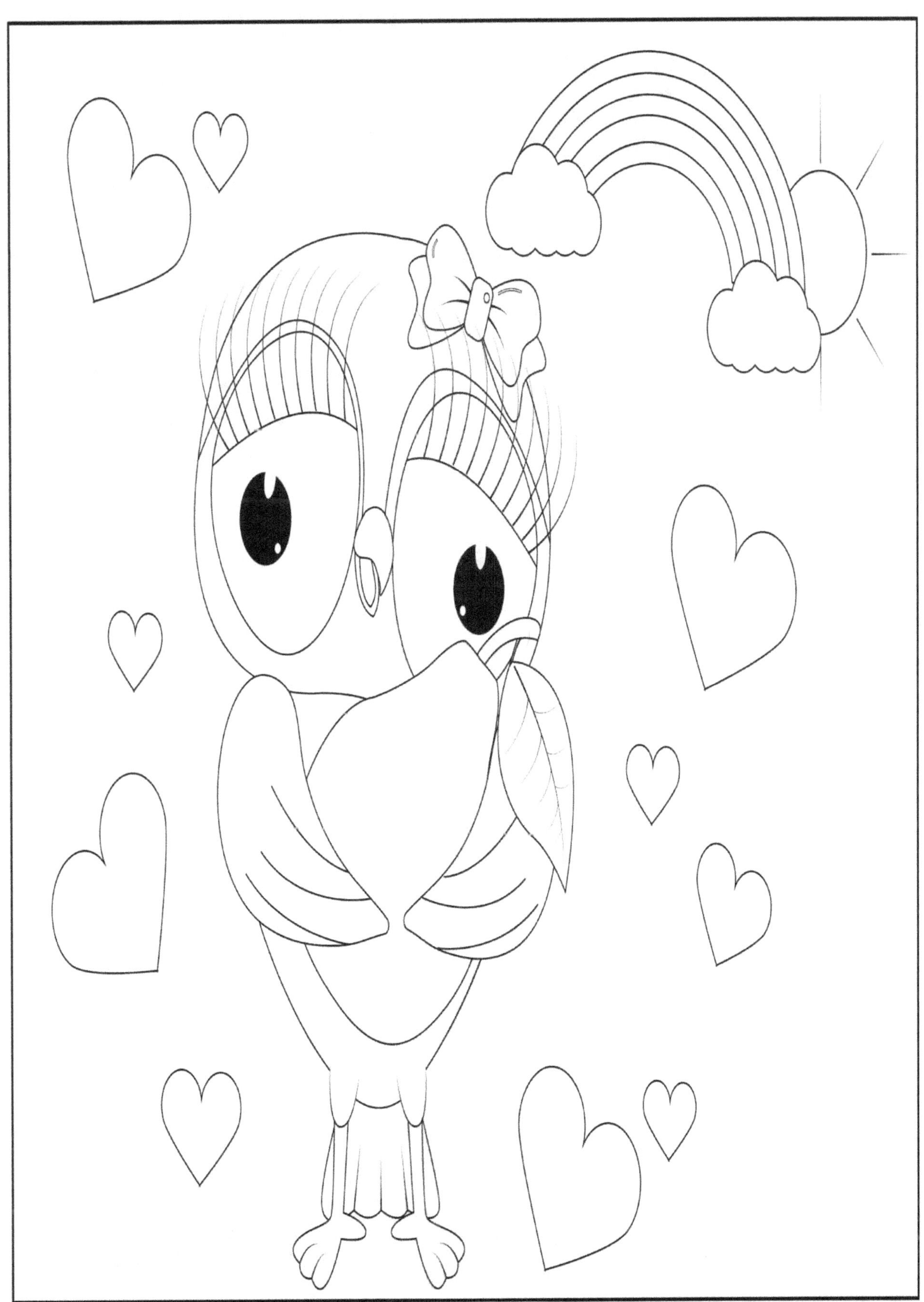

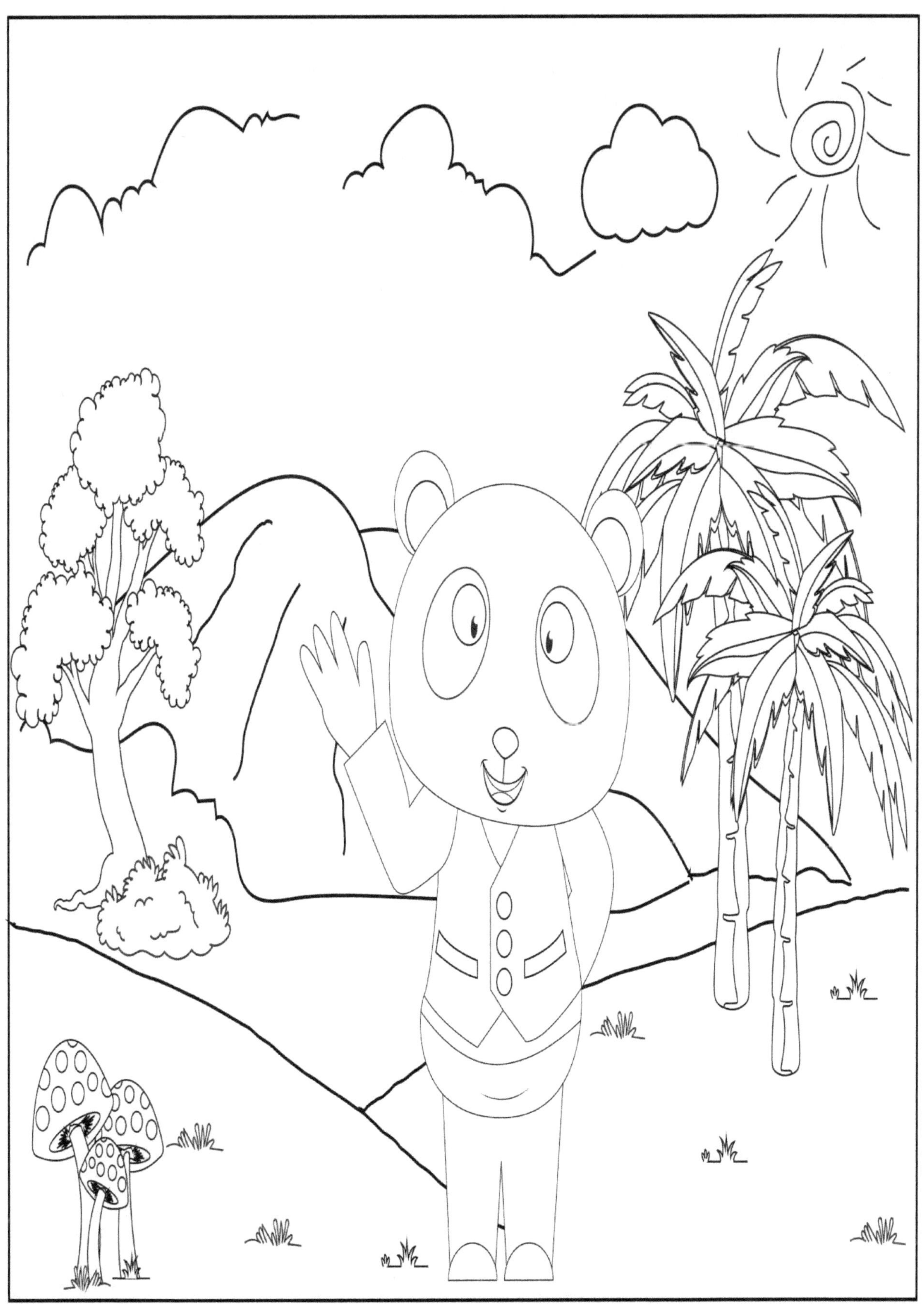

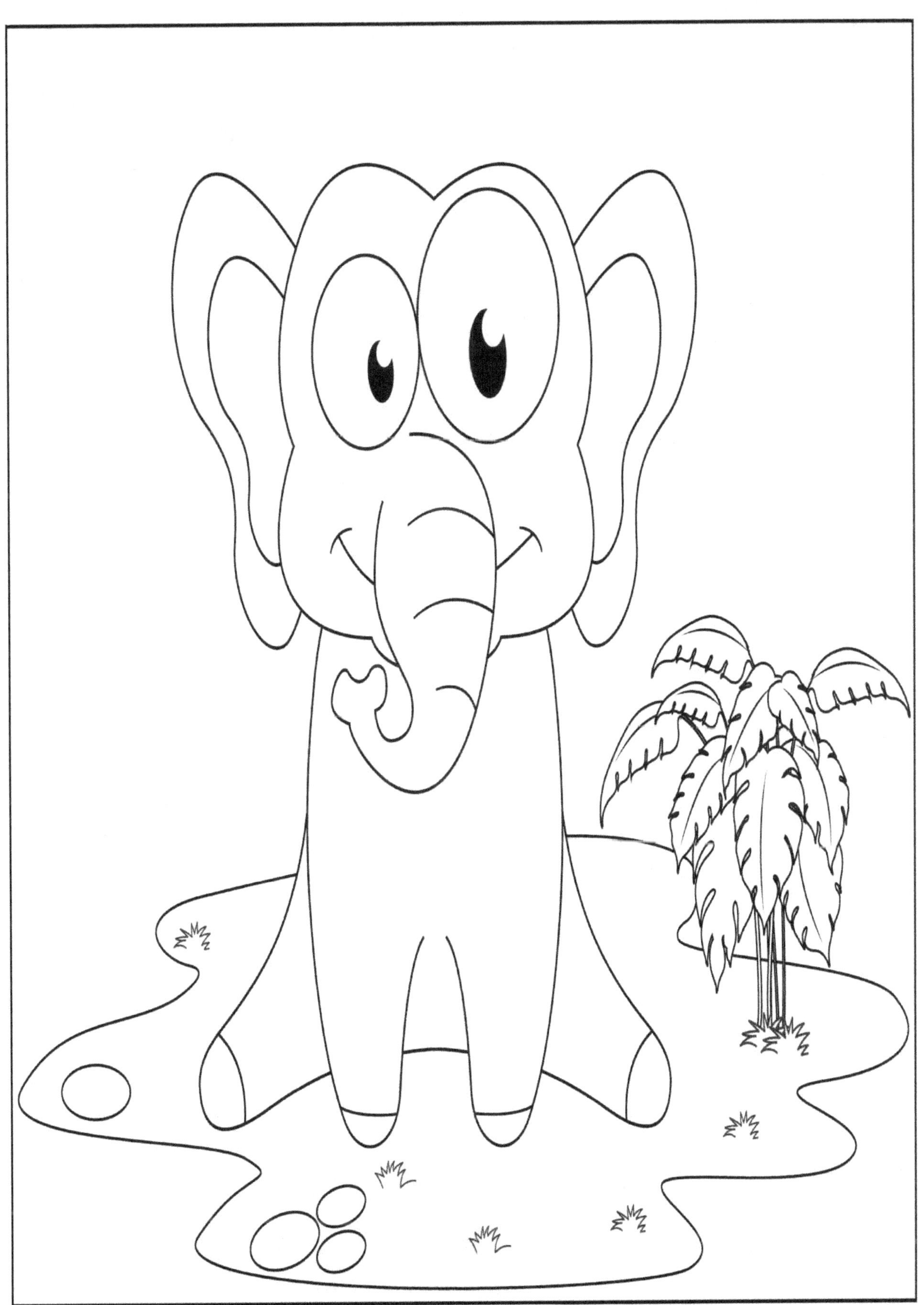

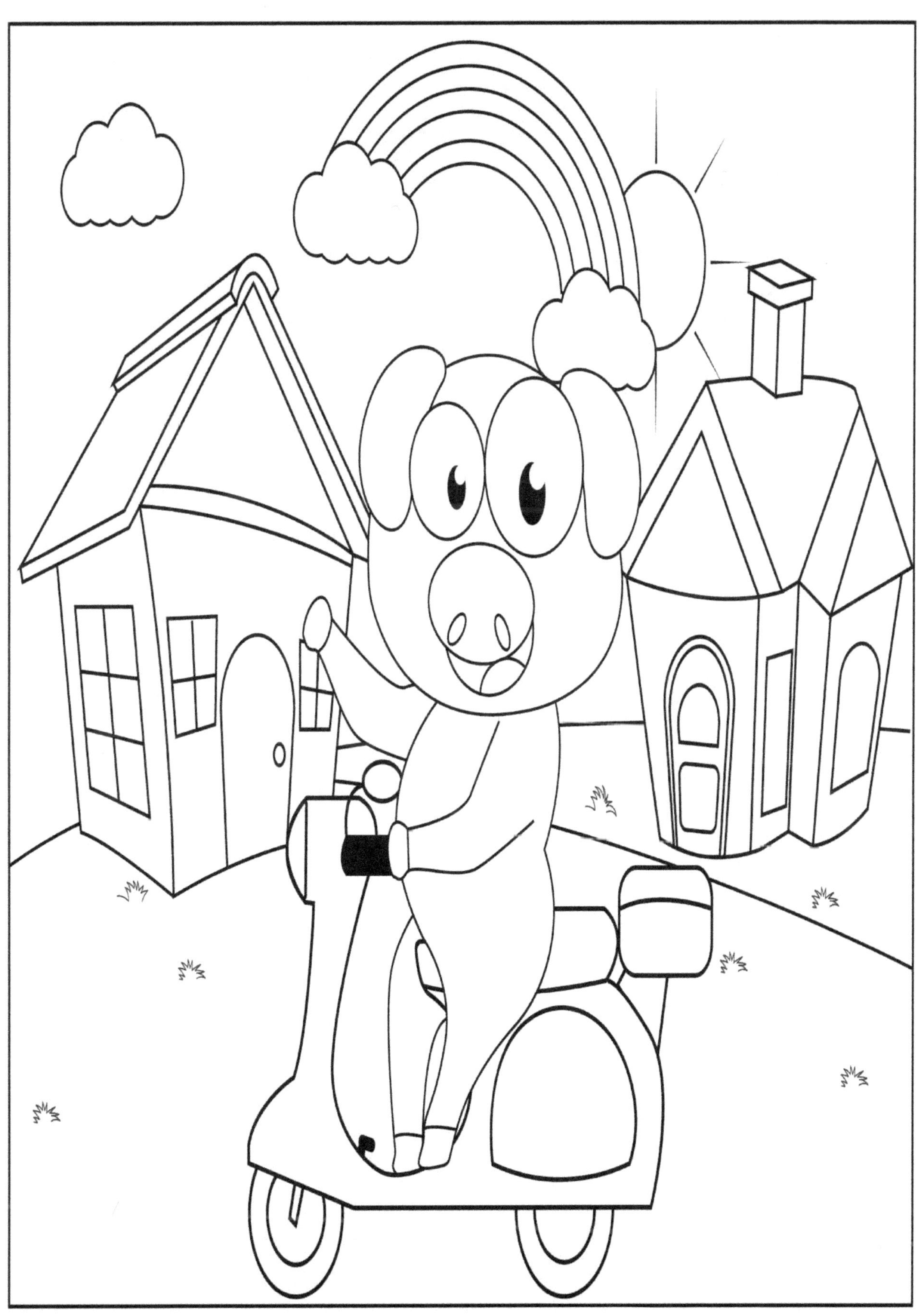

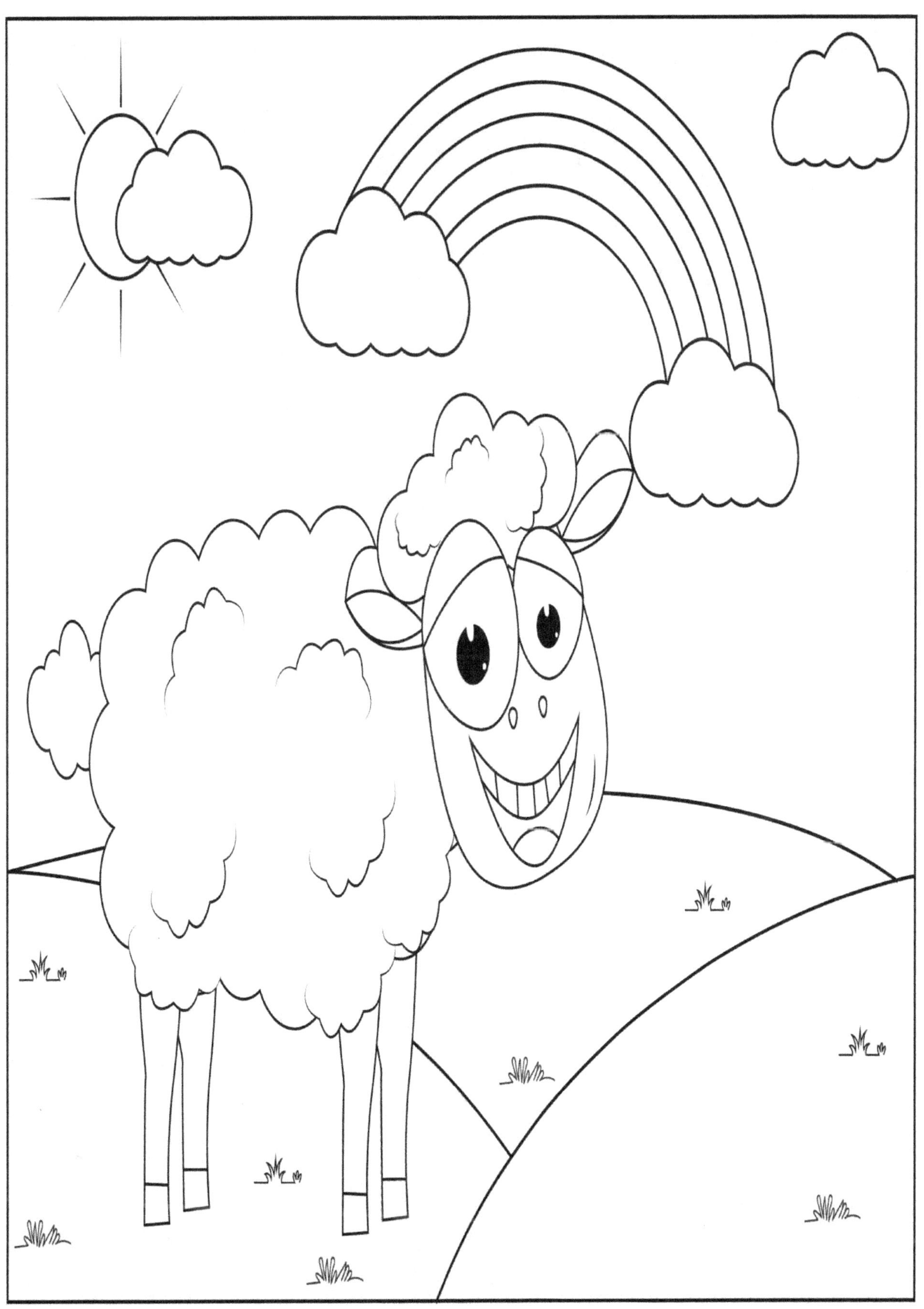

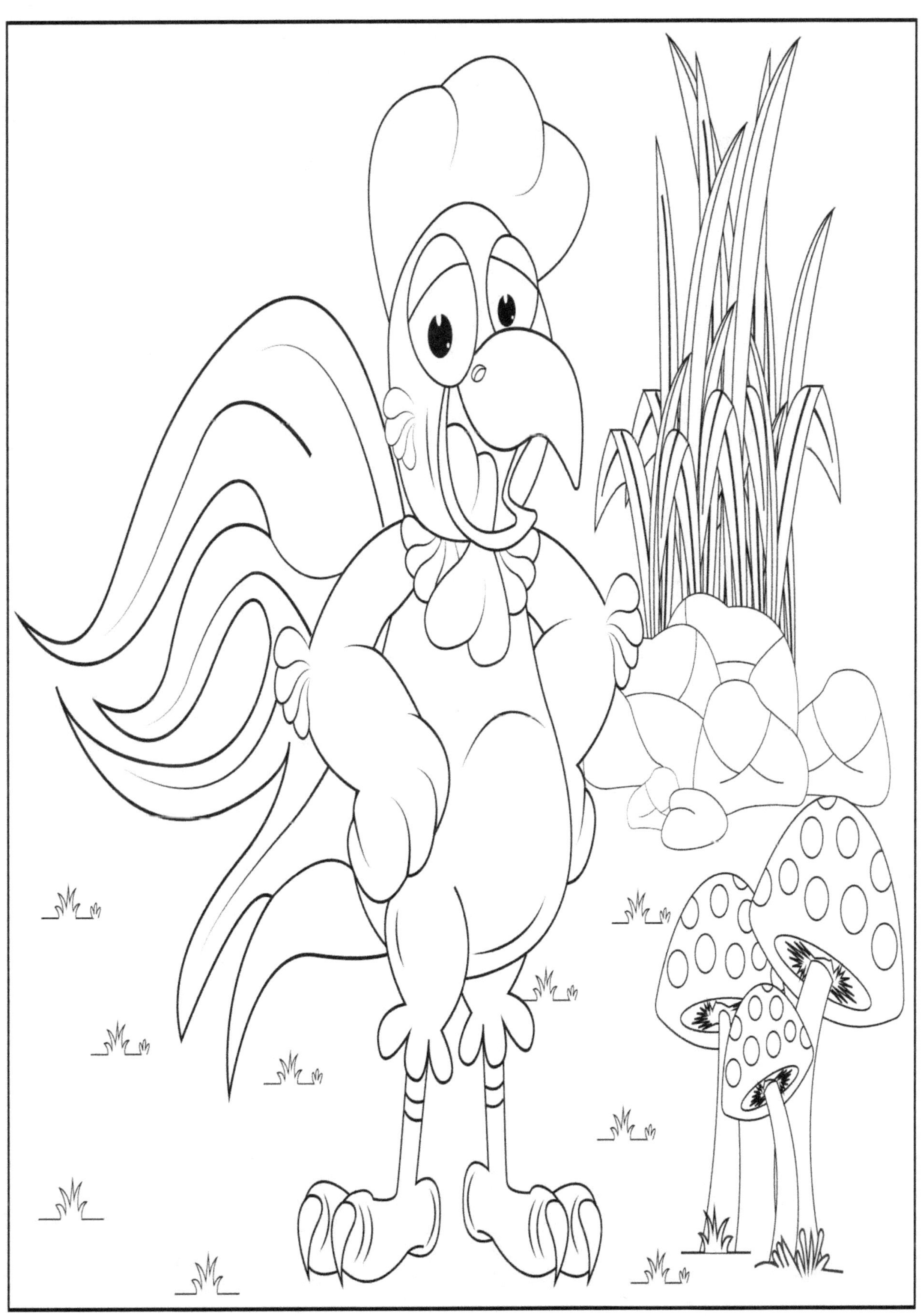

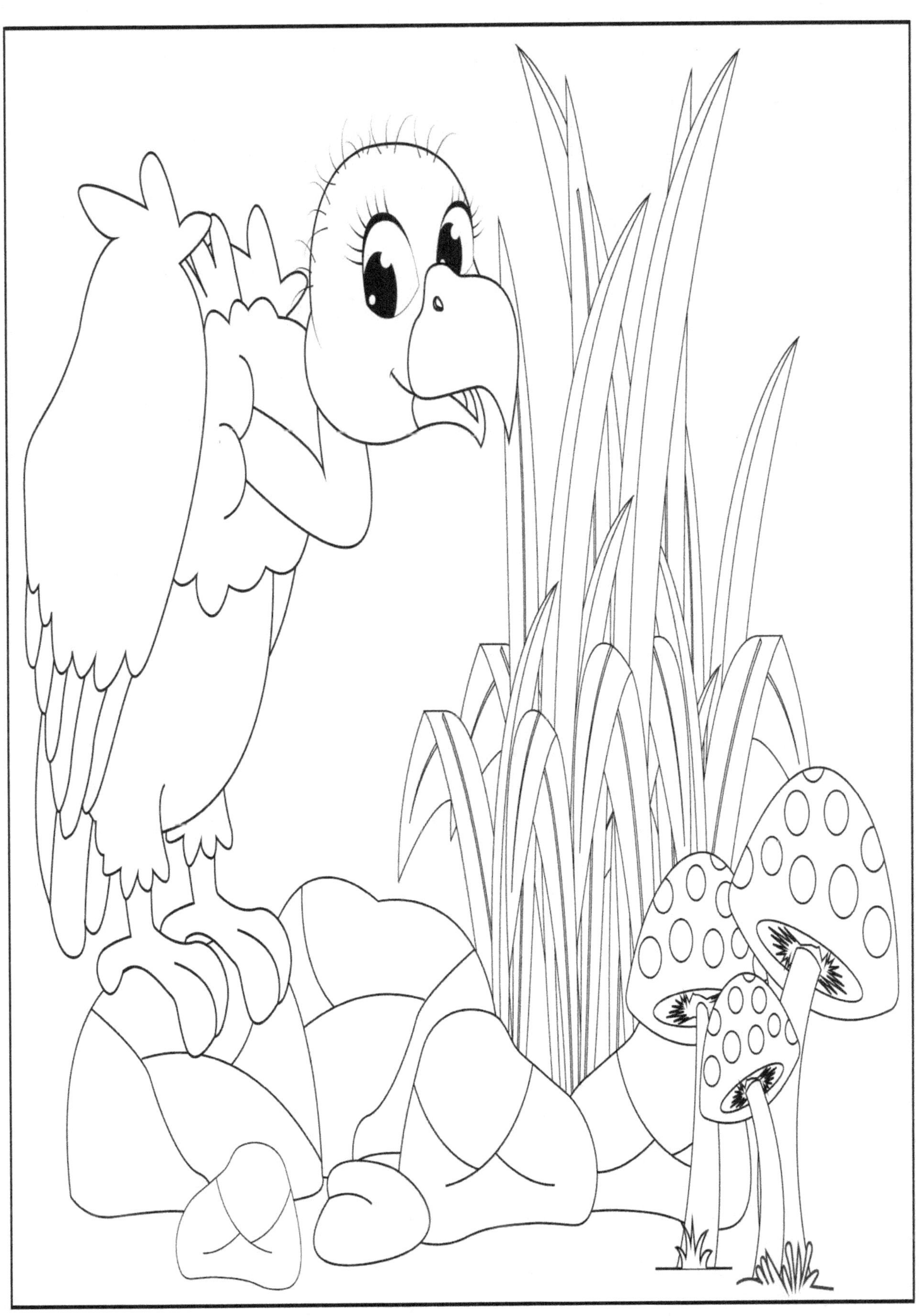

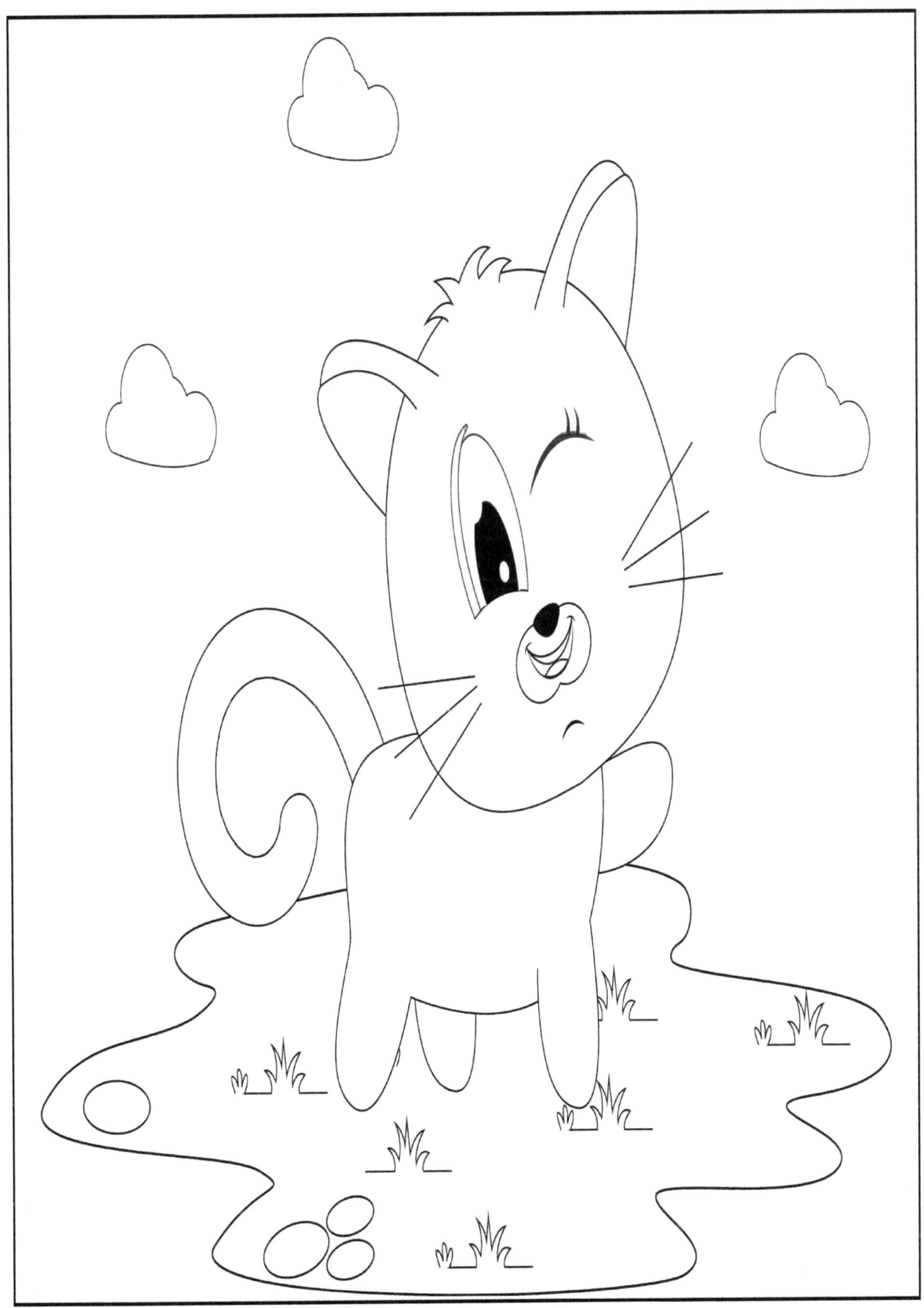

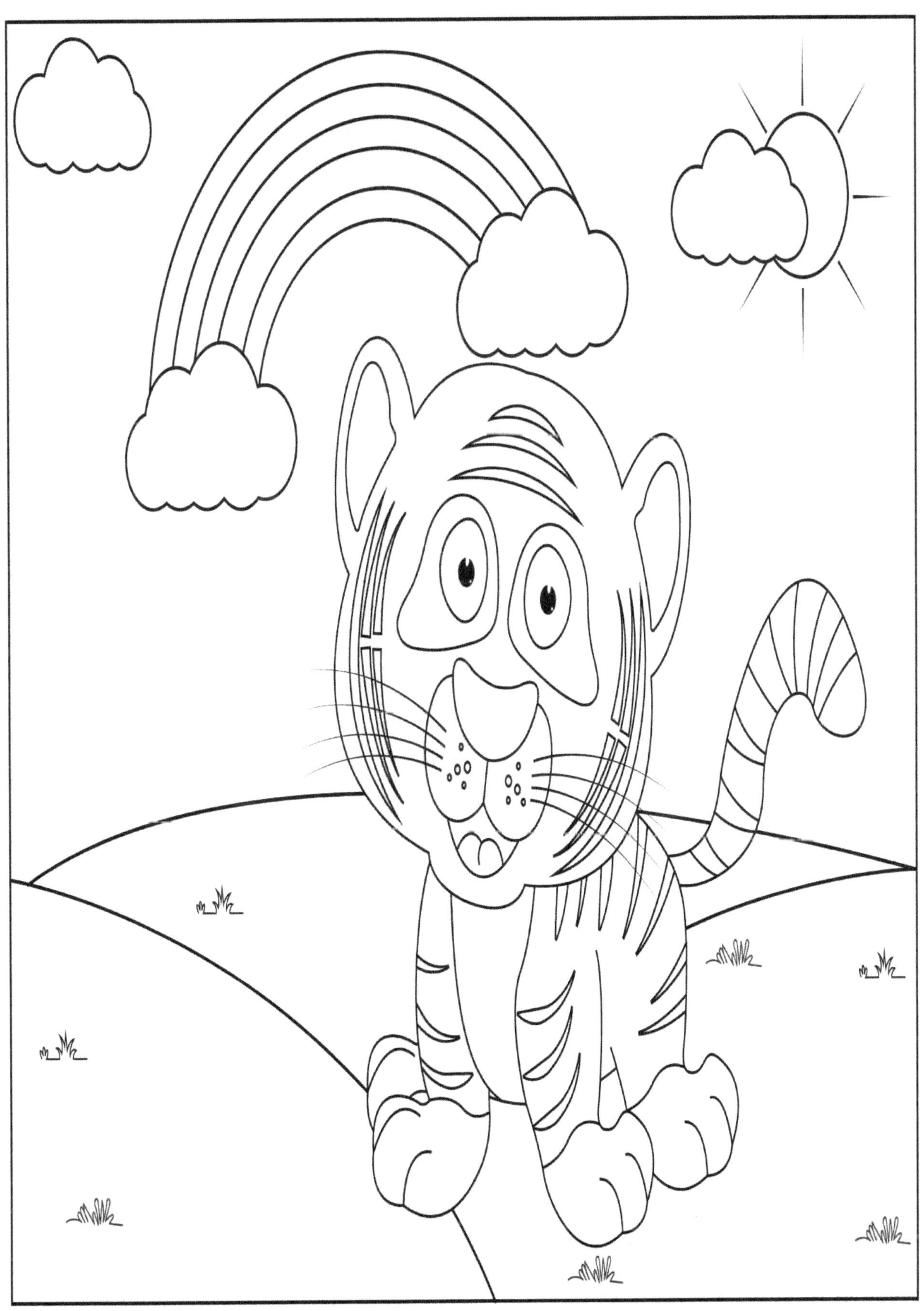

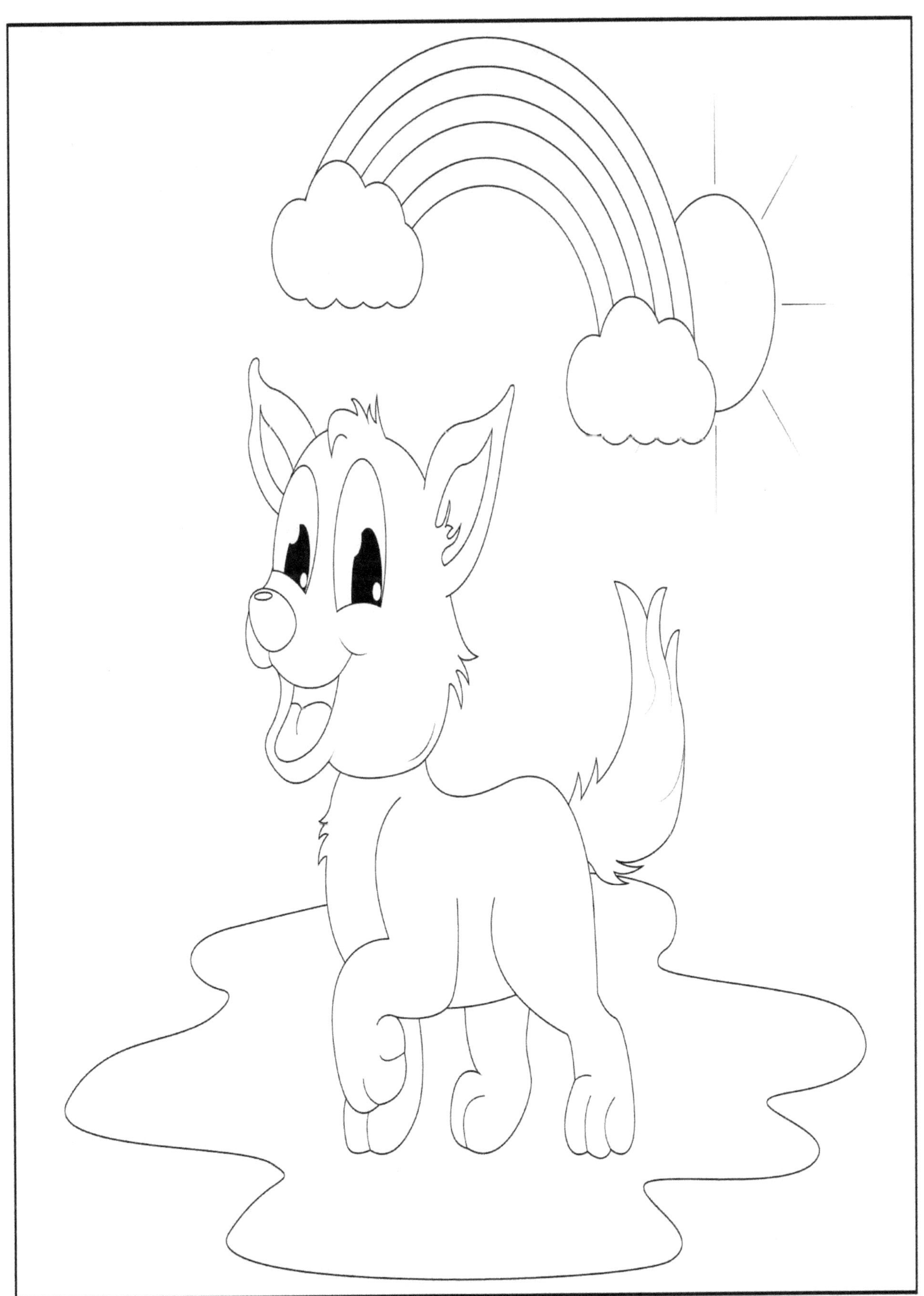

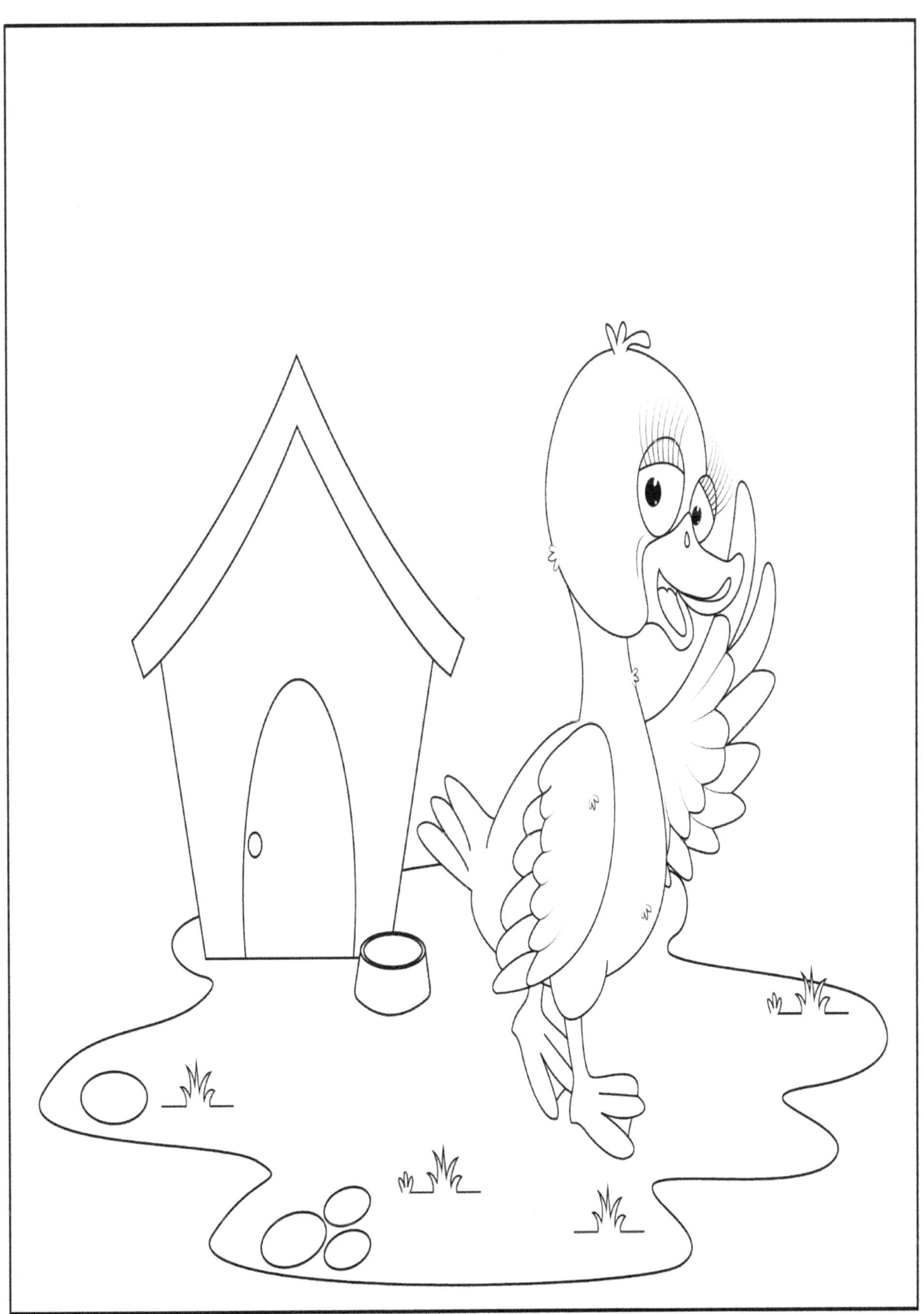

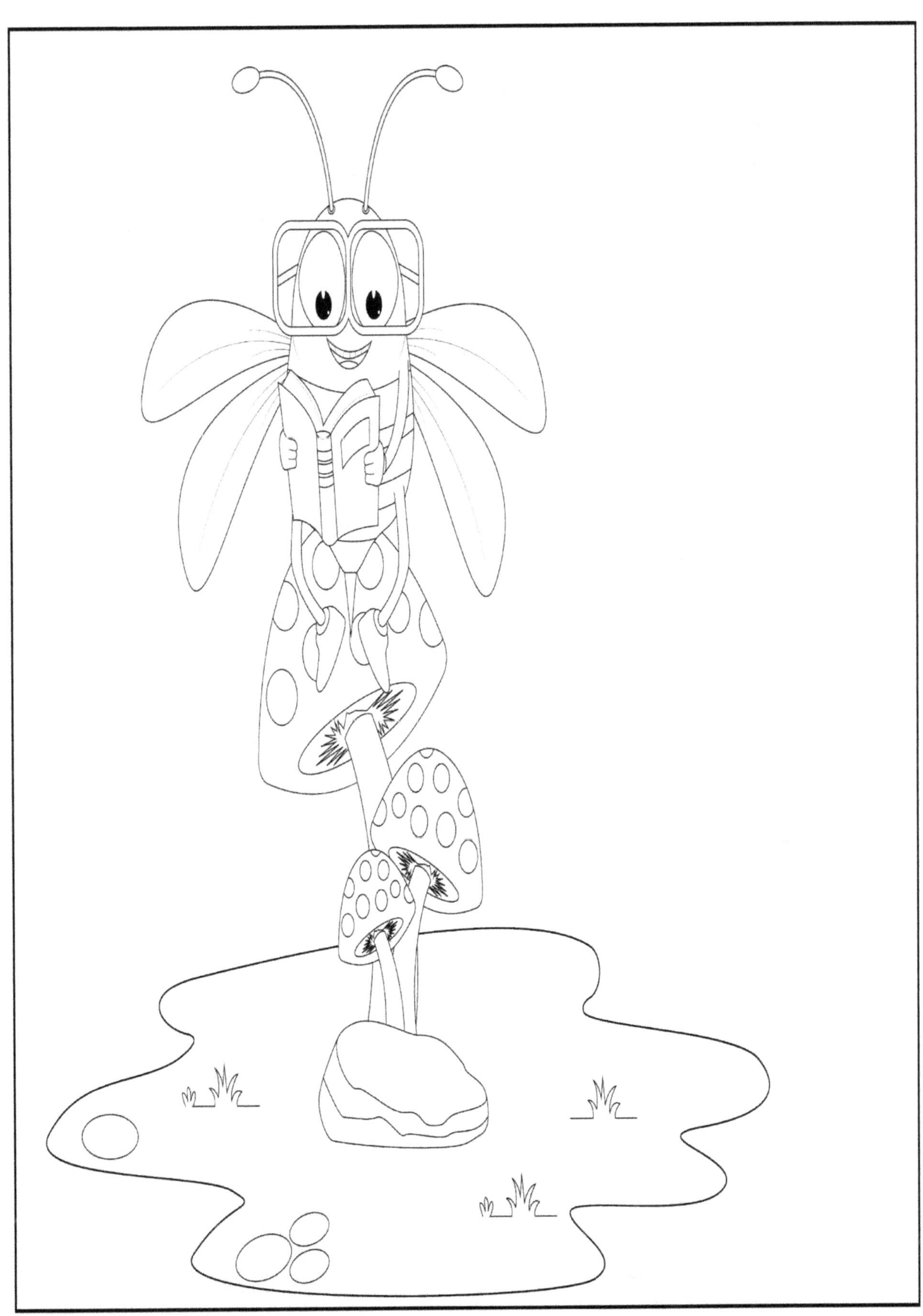

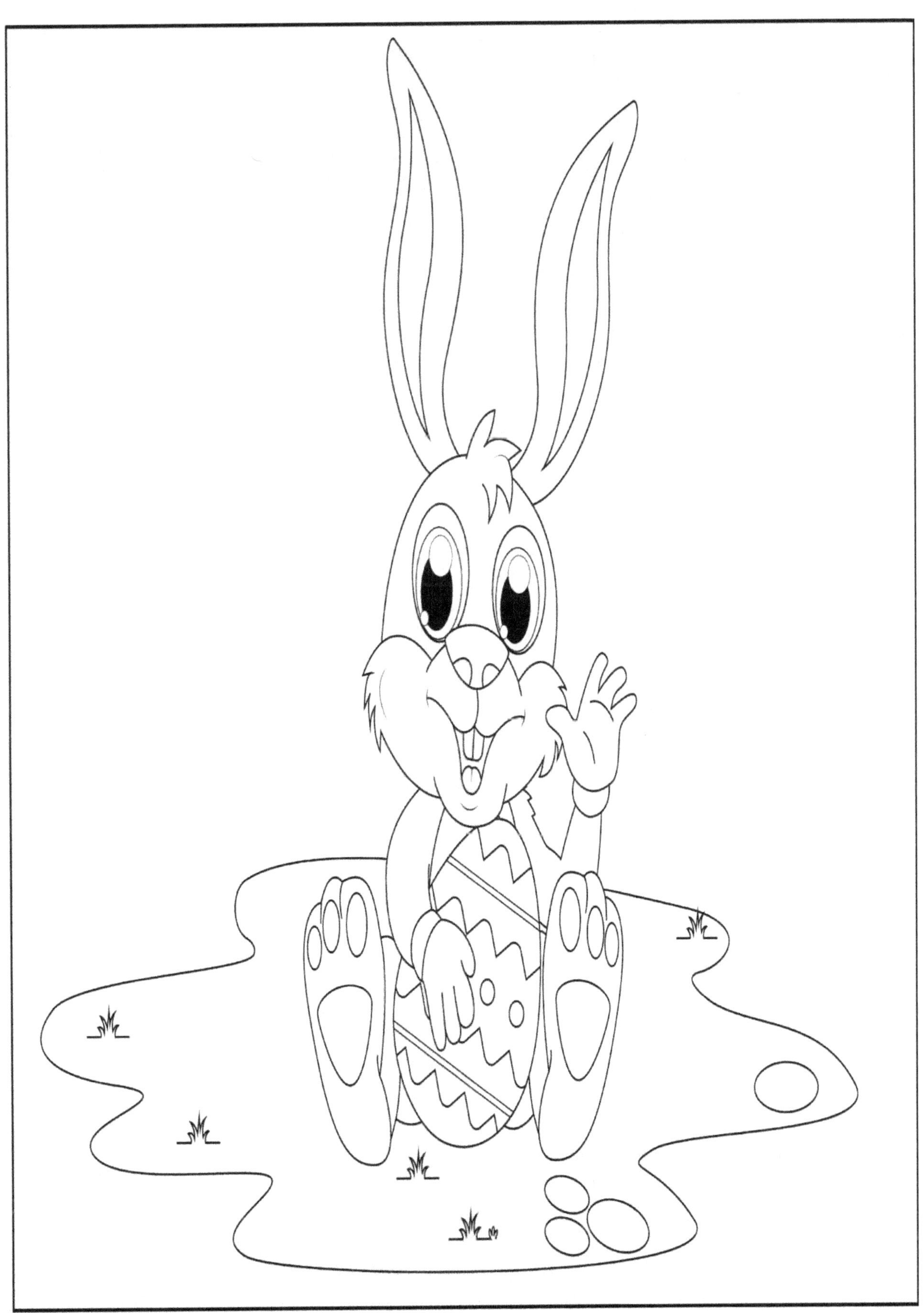

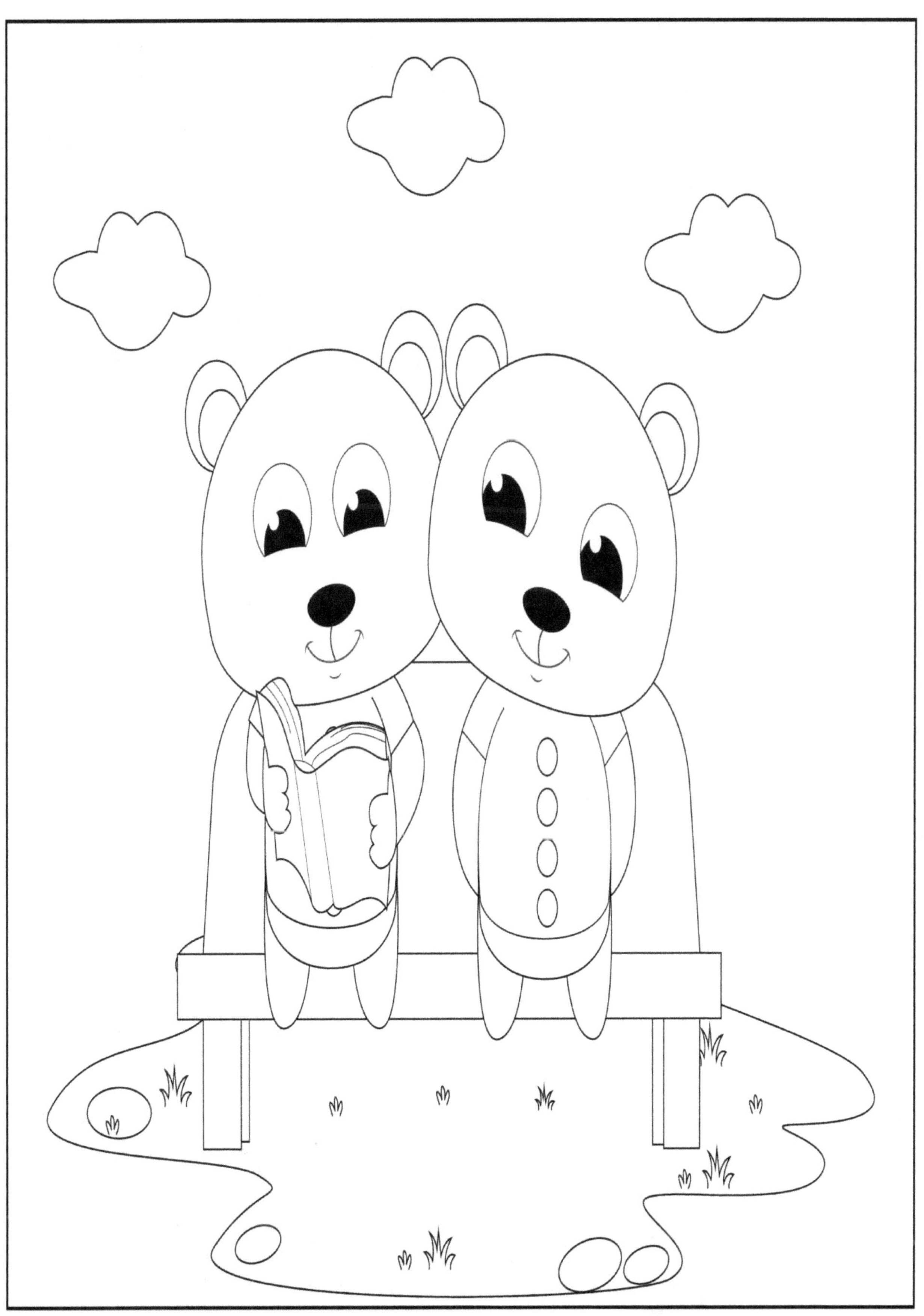

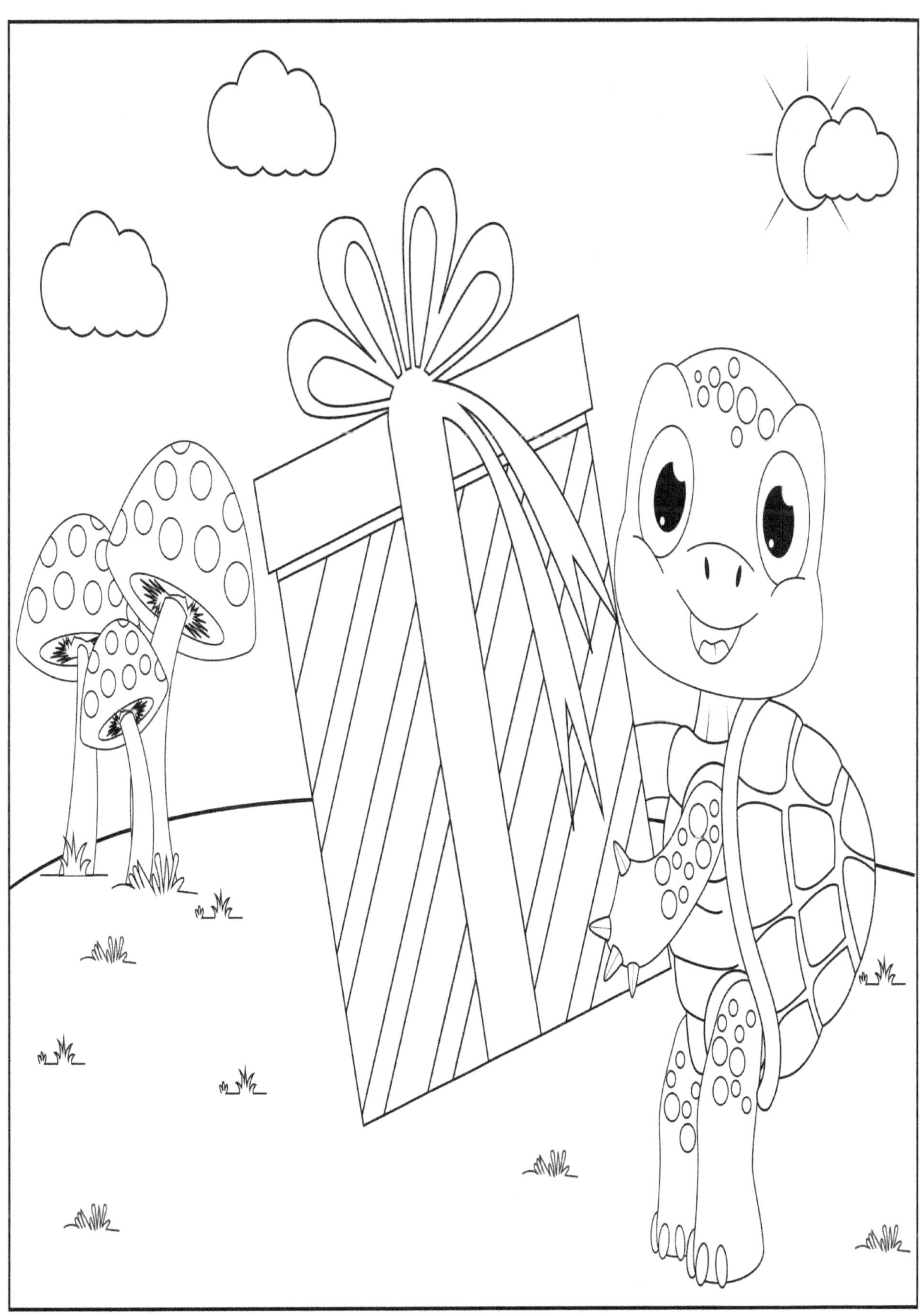